Report Writing

Report Writing

Joan van Emden

and

Jennifer Easteal

McGRAW-HILL Book Company (UK) Limited

London · New York · St Louis · San Francisco · Auckland · Bogotá
Guatemala · Hamburg · Johannesburg · Lisbon · Madrid · Mexico
Montreal · New Delhi · Panama · Paris · San Juan · São Paulo
Singapore · Sydney · Tokyo · Toronto

Published by

McGRAW-HILL Book Company (UK) Limited
MAIDENHEAD · BERKSHIRE · ENGLAND

British Library Cataloguing in Publication Data
Van Emden, Joan
  Report writing.
  1. Report writing
  I. Title II. Easteal, Jennifer
  808'.066   PE1478

  ISBN 0-07-084985-4

Library of Congress Cataloging-in-Publication Data
van Emden, Joan.
  Report writing.

  Bibliography: p.
  1. Report writing. I. Easteal, Jennifer.
II. Title.
PE1478.V28 1987   808'.0666   86-21451
ISBN 0-07-084985-4

12345 CUP 8987 $808 \atop ·066$ 10005843

Typeset by J & K Hybert, Design & Type, Maidenhead, Berkshire SL6 4JP.
Printed in Great Britain by Whitstable Litho Ltd., Whitstable, Kent

Contents

Preface

If a report does not attract the reader, it will not be effective. An individual or a company may produce excellent, original work, but if the presentation, writing and layout of the report do not equal the quality of the content, reader goodwill is lost, and the report itself may be ignored or its author's technical competence, often unjustly, called into question.

We have for several years been aware of the shortage of suitable texts on the subject. The Institution of Electrical Engineers commissioned us to write their Professional Brief on *Technical Report Writing*, and the demand for copies when it was published encouraged us in writing this book, covering the subject more widely and including case study material. The quotations, examples and case studies are almost all 'real-life', and we are grateful to the many companies and organizations, necessarily anonymous, who have allowed us to use their material in this way. The case studies have been used on some of our courses, and provided useful and, we believe, entertaining practice in the writing of reports.

Two comments remain. First, we are aware that report writers can be male or female, but to avoid the awkward repetition of 'he or she', we have used 'he' consistently. Second, other lecturers in Communication Studies have commented on the lack of material available, and we hope that they, and anyone who has to write reports in the course of his job, will find this book helpful and stimulating.

Reading College of Technology
1987

Joan van Emden
Jennifer Easteal

Acknowledgements

Joan van Emden and Jennifer Easteal are grateful to the following for information supplied and for assistance given in the preparation of this book: George Easteal; Colin Grey, Department of Construction Management, Reading University; Elizabeth Johnson and Dr Gillian van Emden, Department of Pure and Applied Zoology, Reading University; Dr Paul H. Scott; Professor Wolfgang van Emden. Any factual errors which remain are our own.

We are grateful for the cooperation of a wide range of companies and organizations who have asked to remain anonymous but who kindly supplied examples, and to all the course delegates and students on whom we have tried out our ideas and our material. We also thank Ann Redfern and Lorraine Standing for their careful preparation of the typescript.

Acknowledgement is also made to: The Royal Institution of Chartered Surveyors for permission to quote from the report, *Life Cycle Costing for Construction*; The Motor Industry Information Service of the Society of Motor Manufacturers and Traders, for permission to use their statistics.

CHAPTER 1

Report production: making decisions

'All the world's a stage', remarked Jaques in *As You Like It*, and after that lively and attractive introduction to his subject, he outlined with commendable clarity the seven parts played by each individual actor, concluding with the even more memorable (if slightly melancholy) lines about second childhood, dentures and bifocals. His, or rather Shakespeare's, reporting technique is brilliant: the introduction, the logical progression, the strong conclusion. Whatever the form of report we shall discuss in this book, that pattern should be followed. Shakespeare also wrote for his audience, knowing what they would expect, accept, and be excited by: this too is a rule of good report writing. As we have written elsewhere[1], the first of such rules is:

> The reader is the most important person.

So the craft of producing a good report demands two particular skills: getting to know the reader, and organizing the information for him. It no doubt also helps if the writer is a genius, but geniuses are rare in the field of report writing, and much will be forgiven the writer who abides by these two criteria. He must also be sure what kind of report he is working on.

The simplest form of report is a memo, which may even be handwritten. It is the least formal, shortest report, usually written from one colleague to another. For instance, Alan goes to a meeting at which he picks up a piece of information which might be useful to Jim, who is away on holiday. Sensibly realizing that by the time Jim comes back, he, Alan, will probably have forgotten all about the incident, he writes a memo on the company memo paper, with its printed heading of To, From, Date and Subject. Alan knows his reader (it's Jim, who has worked in the same building for the last five years; they sometimes have a pint together in the pub after work), and he knows that Jim will be interested in what he has to say. So he organizes his material. Remembering his Shakespeare, he starts with an introduction ('You remember that paper by Joe Bloggs you said was useful for the Zeugma Project? I met Joe Bloggs at the conference in Edinburgh a few days ago...'). Having attracted Jim's attention, Alan gives him the useful information in a logical form ('He says he's got another paper on the same topic coming out in a few weeks' time, and he'll send you an offprint. If you're going to the European conference in Brussels in July, he would like to meet you there and have a chat'). The conclusion is short, to the point and friendly. ('I hope this is useful. See you next week.') The memo is a report, for Jim's benefit, on a small piece of information discovered by Alan. It is sensibly constructed in three short paragraphs (the final one being only two brief sentences), and it is written in an informal style (it will be dated, as all reports should be, but probably just signed 'Alan').

This is an extreme example of a report, indeed, it is only just worth calling a report. At the other extreme, there is the kind of report produced by international agencies, perhaps by a body of the United Nations Organization, in 15 leather-bound volumes, beautifully printed with coloured maps and expensively produced diagrams, and with a Volume 16 which is (mercifully) a Summary. The organization responsible for such a report has also considered its readership, which may be worldwide and using English only as a common language. It has also organized vast amounts of abstruse material into a complex (but not over-complicated) and logical system, and its style is very formal. Reports, with the single exception of the little memo-report, are formal documents, and their organization (Chapter 3) and language (Chapter 4) must reflect this formality.

In between these extremes is a wide range of reports, including laboratory reports, accident reports, progress reports, final advisory reports, and visit reports (the kind of report which might be produced by an engineer after a site visit abroad to investigate local problems in the use of machinery supplied by his company). Each type of report presents its own challenge, but all must adhere to the principles outlined at the start of the chapter: *the needs of the reader are all-important*, and *the material must be clearly and logically organized*. Later in this book, report structure will be discussed and guidelines for differing formats will be suggested. In the case studies (p. 85 onwards), information is supplied which can be organized into different kinds of reports or sections of reports. In the remainder of this chapter, we will look at the identification of the reader's needs and at the decisions which have to be made within the report writer's own organization.

Report readers are few in number; report users are numerous. As most report writers are also report users, it is perhaps surprising that this distinction is so often overlooked. The report reader starts at the beginning of the report and works his way through it to the end, after which he will probably turn into a report user. The more frequently-met user looks at the beginning of the report and reads a few pages, turns to the end of the report and reads a bit more, and then goes to the contents list to choose which sections he will read in detail. He may not read the sections he chooses in order, and he may never read some of the report at all. In making his decision, he will be guided by what is useful to him, and the writer must therefore make sure that attention is drawn to the most important information: the conclusions and/or recommendations, given in brief at the beginning and in detail towards the end, and particular sections which can be identified easily by the individual reader. Such sections must not only be identifiable, but must also be logically placed so that the overall pattern of the report is clear.

The writer of reports must, then, identify his reader: sometimes the identification is obvious (he is a more senior officer within the organization); sometimes he is the representative of a client company (identifiable but not personally known); sometimes, and frighteningly, he is a range of people (some technically qualified and some not). All of these may have to take decisions on the basis of the information in the report. While there can be no absolute rules about how much to find out, the writer should make every attempt to discover who the *principal* reader is (often, the one who controls expenditure), what his technical expertise might be and how it differs from the writer's own, what level of technical language is acceptable, and what other expertise will be available to him. It is also important to know what his interest is: is he being asked to spend money, sign a contract, agree to further investigation, accept that the machinery is tested to approved standards of safety? What does the reader want to know, and what is he likely to do with the information? Any other details which might help the writer, for instance whether the two companies, the writer's and the reader's, have worked together successfully in the past, or whether English is the reader's usual working language, should be noted and remembered throughout the production of the report. All such information will be helpful in getting the tone right.

'Tone' is difficult to define, but it is the 'getting it right for the reader' aspect of report production which is all-important. It includes understanding of the reader's point of view, the logical organization of material, clear and accurate writing, helpful and well-produced diagrams and a contents list which will guide the report user to the most important information. Less obviously, it also includes choosing a binding which will allow diagrams to lie flat, and which will not disintegrate if the report is handled frequently. A type size which is easy to read and not too small (10 point rather than 8 point), paper which will stand up to heavy use (grease-resistant if it is to be used in workshops), a cover which attracts attention without being garish (perhaps using the company colour) all help to make good 'tone'. The reader should *want* to use the report because it looks attractive, and should be encouraged to read on because the physical reading is made as easy as possible. It is surprising how often potential readers are put off by unnumbered pages crowded with small print. If the report is expensive to produce and influential in content, it is often worth employing a consultant designer to present the material effectively and to ensure its maximum impact.

Knowing the reader is important; understanding the writer's own organization is also helpful. Decisions have to be made which may militate against much good advice given in this book: time is frequently short, so that checking is inadequate; responsibilities are not clarified so that page or diagram numbers are lost between the report writer and his secretary; senior staff may take control and change the emphasis of a report written by a more junior employee who may nevertheless know more about the particular problem, or the individual reader, than those above him do. The writer must beware the pitfalls of his own company, one of which can be a conflict within the terms of reference for a report. Different senior staff want different documents: a briefing document to be used at a meeting, a formal report which can be shown to a client, a specification or manual which could be back-up to other information. The junior report writer must, even at the cost of being temporarily unpopular, establish what sort of document he is being asked to produce, and what its use will be. Lack of clear guidance may lead to a report which attempts to do different and even conflicting jobs, and the resulting confusion can lead to the temporary unpopularity becoming permanent.

Time available for the draft version and for the final stage on the word processor should both be made clear to the writer: it can be very frustrating to rush a report through to its apparent completion and then to discover ten days later that the officer responsible for validating it and authorizing distribution hasn't moved it from his in-tray. The appropriate length of the finished document should also be clarified: this may be a 'political' consideration dependent on the cost of the report. The newcomer to an organization needs to ask questions about procedure, restriction, authorization, availability of computer or word processor time and, most of all, about guidelines. Looking at past reports within the company is helpful, but a set of short, well-illustrated guidelines (sometimes produced as a 'dummy report') showing exactly what the company demands and where flexibility is allowed, should be given to every new employee who is likely to write reports. His attention might also be drawn to the copy of this book in the company library, with a recommendation to purchase his own with part of his new salary. Report writers need all the help they can get!

CHAPTER 2

Preparation

Most reports are exercises in persuasion. They exist to sell a product, an idea or a point of view, and, if they are successful, they result in action being taken, whether it is the development of a new project or the introduction of advanced safety procedures. Some reports review a whole industry in the light of competition from abroad; other reports show how a new system of lighting could improve working conditions for typists, or safety in a workshop; yet other reports show how efficiency could be increased or money could be saved. Apart perhaps from accident reports, which should 'describe what happened' without prejudice, and laboratory reports, which describe the methods used and the results of experiments, most reports are subjective.

This, of course, contradicts the general feeling that reports should look objectively and dispassionately at a problem, and become 'personal' only in making recommendations. Yet in reality, both points of view are true. The facts presented in a report should be exactly that: facts, without bias or comment. Only in the light of such evidence can conclusions be accurately drawn and wise recommendations made. At the same time, no report writer presents every aspect of every piece of information he finds out: he makes choices, in the light of the reader's need and to a certain extent his own need too. In being selective in the facts he presents, he is inevitably making personal decisions, and in organizing these facts he is making subjective judgements. It is important for report writers to be aware of this, for to acknowledge one's own prejudices or to face the inadequacy of the information available is to take stock of the report potential and to allow for possible weaknesses in report presentation.

Objectives

Nevertheless, the report writer must start from a clear perception of his reader's needs and of his own terms of reference. The previous chapter has shown the importance of understanding as much as possible of the reader's or report user's outlook, and it also suggested some of the considerations, such as time available, which must be kept in mind. The terms of reference of a report also show what type of document has to be produced, and its objective, that is, what the writer hopes will happen as a result of his work. He needs to be sure about this, and it is often helpful to write out the objective in a sentence or two before more detailed work begins. Sometimes there are double objectives, one to gain further support for the project under consideration and the other, confidential to the writer, to impress the reader so much that promotion/a bonus/the offer of a better job, will follow. Again, it is best that the writer is aware of such mixed motives (not necessarily conflicting), even though only one is declared. Questions, honestly asked and honestly answered, help to clarify the objective(s):

1. What does the reader know about this subject?

2. What does the reader want to know?

3. What do I want the reader to know about this subject?

4. Is there a discrepancy between (2) and (3), and if so, what is its importance?

5. What action does the reader expect to take as a result of this report?

6. What action do I want the reader to take as a result of this report?

7. Is there a discrepancy between (5) and (6), and if so, what is its importance, to the reader and to me?

8. Why am I (not anybody else) writing this particular report for this particular reader? (This questions may well already have been answered, but it may also pinpoint specific requirements.)

When the identity of the reader and the objective of the report are clear, the report writer needs again to review any special considerations: time has been mentioned; the cost of any investigations needed may also have to be kept in mind; sometimes confidentiality will be a constant problem, limiting the information sought or included. There may also be reference books which should be available: previous reports, comparative figures, relevant British Standards, company guidelines and, not least, good English and perhaps also technical dictionaries. The writer is now prepared for action, and indeed information may already be arriving on his desk.

Collection of facts

There can be no set procedure for collecting the facts needed for a report. In some cases, experiments in the laboratory and their measured results will provide enough material for a report; at other times, interviews, site visits, detailed measurements and calculations may be needed to supplement background reading. In one of the case studies in this book (the Morgan Report, p. 105), the procedure itself perhaps presents the greatest difficulty: how does one find out what people think about the management of their

6

company? Certainly, asking them is unlikely to be very helpful. Whatever the procedure necessary to ascertain the facts, it must be followed as fully as possible, however difficult or unpromising any particular line of enquiry might seem. Within the limits set down in the terms of reference, the facts must be discovered.

Preliminary organization

The result of such a relentless search is often a heap of material of differing usefulness. Some preliminary sorting out is needed. At an early stage, it is helpful to work on the basis of three categories of information. Category A material is in the mainstream of the report, obviously relevant to the subject and crucial to the report's success; Category B contains material probably useful as back-up, or for some specialized readers, or helpful but not essential to the understanding of the report; Category C is the place for information which has been unearthed during the investigation and which is not uninteresting, but which has dubious relevance to the report as a whole. It would be unwise to jettison the third category at this stage, as subsequent findings might make apparently irrelevant material much more important than at first appears. Flexibility is important, and so information might move between all three categories until it finds the right permanent place. In the end, Category A material will probably become the main body of the report, Category B material might become an appendix or appendices, and Category C will either be put away for another time or fill the wastepaper basket.

When the information for the whole report, or for a major section of it, has been collected, it must be organized. Detailed headings and appropriate notation are discussed later, but the first stages of linking ideas and forming patterns can start, and this valuable preparation should not be rushed or omitted: it will make subsequent work much easier to complete. One of the traditional ways of organizing material is to list notes down a page of A4 paper and to draw arrows from one item to another which seems to be connected to it. The result is usually a length of intertwined arrows which becomes increasingly complex as new links between pieces of information are found. There is still, in spite of all the arrows, the inherent problem that the writer tends to see the items at the top of the list as more important than the items below it. In merely listing ideas, he has predetermined an order from which it is difficult to escape.

Spider diagrams

An increasingly popular alternative to the list is the Spider Diagram (which has other names such as Brain Pattern[2]). This method of organizing material is not easy to work with at the first attempt, and we, the authors, would stress that some perseverance is needed (but we found that using the system soon became easier and now we couldn't manage without it!). The process of forming a spider diagram starts with a brainstorming session. One key word, or perhaps key phrase, is written randomly on the page to represent each idea or item to be included in the report. It may be helpful not to use the standard A4 format, but to turn the page through 90° so that the page shape itself is unusual (wide rather than deep) and ruled lines become irrelevant. The main key word, the theme of the whole report, can then be placed in the centre of the page, and other key words radiate from the centre in any direction and with no discernible hierarchy. Each idea is enclosed in its 'bubble', and the 'bubbles' can then be linked by lines as appropriate. A simple example (see Figure 2.1) might produce a checklist for a speaker at a conference; he records in a random fashion the details he must remember:

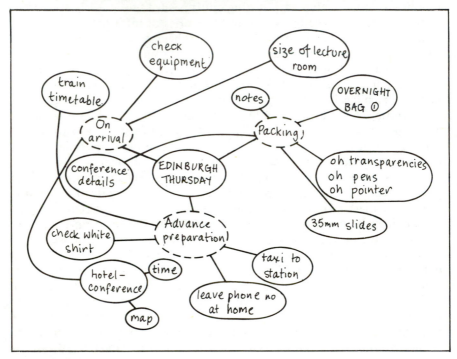

Figure 2.1 *Spider diagram for conference*

Working from the central 'bubble', 'EDINBURGH THURSDAY', the speaker can organize his ideas in three sections, by linking the items which are 'advance preparation' (getting a train timetable, ordering the taxi to the station, etc.), those which involve 'packing' (his overnight bag and the equipment he needs for his presentation), and those which he will have to deal with on arrival, such as finding his way from the hotel to the conference centre and timing the journey. In focusing on each, he will probably notice any 'missing links': he has thoughtfully left his phone number at home, but has forgotten to leave it with his secretary in case of a work crisis during his absence (or perhaps the omission was deliberate). It is always worth considering whether an apparent missing link is the result of lack of research, unobtainable information, or oversight.

One or two items are probably complicated in themselves, and could be the subject of a separate bubble. So, in the example given, 'overnight bag' is not much help when its owner is packing, but it could be given a number (1 in this instance) and subordinate bubble number 1 will then have 'OVERNIGHT BAG' in the centre, with individual items (toothpaste, etc.) radiating from it. Indeed, this subordinate bubble might be standard for all the one-day conferences this speaker addresses.

Once all the ideas are recorded and linked together, their order can be considered. In this simple example, there are three obvious stages which fall into a logical time sequence:

1. Advance preparation

2. Packing

3. On arrival

These 'key' bubbles (indicated by broken circles) have become apparent as the ideas are linked (the ideas being in completed circles). Different colours for different stages of organization are often helpful. Some bubbles clearly generate sub-divisions: 2. Packing contains personal items such as the overnight bag and 'briefcase' property needed at the conference itself, such as overhead transparencies. These items form subordinate bubbles, the equivalent of sub-sections. Each section and sub-section could, in a report, be given a suitable heading and appropriate decimal number (see Chapter 3). The contents list can then be put together and eventually the sections will be written. The writing itself need not begin at the beginning, as each section can be identified and written as a separate entity (although some final checking for consistency will be needed: see Chapter 6). A light crossing-out will mark each completed section or bubble, and illustrations can be noted as belonging to each section of writing.

Illustrations are not the only additional items which can be noted alongside the spider diagram. A useful 'tool' is a clear space of paper on which can be recorded information which must be included in detail and which cannot be summarized in a key word or phrase. Such information might include people's names, amounts of money, formulae or references. It is often helpful to use A3 paper folded in half, with the spider on one half and the detailed notes opposite. However the spider diagram is organized, it will almost certainly look messy and be personal to its owner (it could probably be tidied up for someone else to look at, but this is secondary to its main purpose of helping its creator to organize his ideas). Your colleagues may make unwelcome comments about those who draw lots of 'doodles' on pieces of paper before 'getting down to the job'; ignore them. You are involved in the serious work of preparing the ideas from which your report will eventually be structured and written.

Nevertheless, when the office is full of piles of information and the desk top is crawling with spiders, you may be tempted to start writing. This would be like starting to build before looking at the architect's plans: not impossible, but hazardous. Reports need to be designed, and the structure must be planned in detail before the words can be put in position. Essentially, reports need beginnings and endings, and a logical sequence in between, and the rest of this chapter and Chapter 3 will show how the different departments of a report are joined to make a whole building. In general terms, the stages described are in the order in which the report writer will work at them, from the linking of ideas in the spider diagram to the detailed organization of the summary, title page and references, but the order may vary with the needs of a particular report. Planning, however, is always the first step.

Beginning and end

Beginning at the beginning can have its uses, but the problem as it faces the report writer is to identify the beginning. Boring the reader with a great deal of information which he already knows is as bad as beginning in the middle and so leaving the reader in total confusion about why the report was needed at all. The latter mistake is usually that of the expert who has worked on the subject of the report for most of his adult life: he knows the background and the particular problem so well that he cannot believe that there exists a reader who does not share this knowledge. So, reasonably from his point of view, he assumes understanding and gets straight to the solution of the problem, leaving his reader wondering why it was a problem in the first place.

Making assumptions about the reader or readers of a report is a dangerous activity. The writer of a good report will have checked, before he began to gather information, the technical expertise of the reader, his knowledge of the subject of the report, his experience of the problem under discussion (knowledge being, of course, very different from experience). With this information in mind, the writer can start to plan the beginning of the report, what needs to be explained and what can sensibly be taken for granted, so that the reader is neither patronized nor bewildered. If the writer is sure that much background information is shared, he can indeed start somewhere in the middle, but he must be sure not only that the knowledge is shared with the intended reader, but also that other readers who might be interested are not puzzled by the absence of explanation. Reports may lie in a drawer for a long time, to be taken out by the original reader's successor, and he too must understand what he reads. Knowing who the reader is, who the other likely readers are, and what they all know about the subject, will determine where the report begins.

In the same way, a decision must be made about the end of a report. It is rarely the end of the story: there will be discussions, meetings, perhaps further reports, and action taken as a result of the report when it is presented. Indeed, the experiments themselves may continue, and the project lead on to a further project, so that the point at which the original report finished is no longer clear. The writer must decide how much his reader needs to know, whether the report is a progress report or a final report, what time constraints he must bear in mind, and in the light of these decisions he can close the report, making sure that the reader is aware if there is more to follow.

Between the beginning and the end come the logical stages. These are necessary, as we showed in Chapter 1, to meet the needs of the report user, the person who will pick and choose which sections to read, which to skim, and which to ignore. The general pattern is clear to the writer once his spiders are drawn and the sections of information identified: the detailed format must now be organized for the sake of that all-important person, the reader.

CHAPTER 3

Format

Contents lists

As we discussed at the end of the previous chapter, the organization of a report, its format, must be clearly defined long before the writing begins. From the earliest stages of the work, the writer must think in terms of sections and headings, and one of the first sections to be written will be the contents list. This may seem surprising, but a provisional list of headings produces a guide to the more detailed organization, and it is flexible: the writer can move headings round on a page more easily than he can reorganize whole sections of writing.

First of all, he must return to the spider of the previous chapter. This animal, as described there, is a useful aid to the accumulation of ideas and the formation of links between them. It is also helpful in providing the headings which will appear in the contents list, for a word or phrase often becomes clear as the general summary of an 'area' of spider. At first, these summary words will usually be vague and wide in scope: 'Background', 'Site Visit', 'Results' are adequate to begin with, although they are too imprecise for the final report. A contents list can still be drawn up at this stage, even if it looks in part like this:

Background

    Terms of Reference

    Own previous work $\lessgtr$ $\begin{array}{l}\text{Experimental} \\ \text{Already published}\end{array}$

    Others' published work

    Aim of this investigation

Nobody could pretend that this is an adequate contents list for a report, but it shows the beginning of a plan of action, and a logical pattern for the report to take. If the writer then decides that other people's published work should be considered before the details of his own, he can easily change the order of his headings, which will involve only a moment's work. Changing whole chunks of written report takes much longer. The precision at which the headings must eventually arrive is discussed later in this chapter, and shown in the worked short report (see page 76). Sometimes, the main sections are known to the writer, who can start to pattern his headings and sub-headings easily. For example, the writer of a report on insulation will be aware that when he considers house insulation, he will deal with three main areas: the walls, the windows and the loft. If House Insulation is the third section of the report, the first contents list might be something like:

3. House Insulation

    Walls

            Cavity
            Dry Lining
            Pebble Decking

    Windows

            Double glazing

    Loft

            Types
            Materials used

The section on loft insulation is vague, and more detailed thought will have to be given to the headings later, but the organization is becoming clear. As long as the contents list is subsequently revised and checked regularly, it is a highly important piece of work achieved, and the report writer can feel a sense of satisfaction in just one page which sets out how the report will be organized and the logic of that organization. However, for most report writers, detailed headings are still in the future, and a standard format appropriate to the report is the first stage in the making of the contents.

Headings

The number and type of headings used will be determined by the length, complexity and formality of the report: sometimes Introduction, Findings, Comments will be sufficient. Company rules may make other headings obligatory, or the report material in itself may need specific treatment. For instance, *a pure science laboratory report* might use the following:

Abstract
Introduction (literature and current state of research)
Materials and methods (experimental design)

Results (including both statistics and, if appropriate, comments)
Discussion (of the writer's own data, put in the context of other
    published work)
Conclusions
Summary
References.

A report which examines and considers *a technical process* might have
headings such as:

Introduction (including the background to and reason for the
    investigation)
Summary (including the main recommendations)
Procedure (how the tests were carried out)
Results (facts only)
Discussion (the implications of the testing)
Conclusions (what is acceptable/not acceptable, and why)
Recommendations (based on the conclusions).

If the *report is advisory*, with lengthy factual and discursive material, it may
need the full 'standard' format, which would contain the following sections:

1 Title page
   Acknowledgements
2 Summary
3 Analytical contents list (sections and page numbers)
4 Terms of reference/Introduction (why the report was written, and for
    whom)
   Procedure (how the information was obtained)
5 Findings (the facts which were obtained)
6 Conclusions (the essential considerations which were revealed)
7 Recommendations (what should happen as a result of the report)
   References (books, journals, etc., mentioned in the report)
   Bibliography (other useful background reading)
   Appendices (supplementary material).

All these headings may be omitted or adapted in any individual report, but
they are a useful aid to the writer in suggesting a pattern for the report and
guiding him in the organization. Most everyday reports will not need such
detailed treatment, but a formal, published report might indeed have all the
above sections.

The report writer now has a framework for the report, and some ideas
for headings, probably within the Procedure and Findings sections. Whether
the actual headings Procedure and Findings, or indeed any other of the
headings listed above, are used or not depends on the report. They may
instead turn into a much more precise form of words, closely linked to the

14

report material. It is the pattern represented by the headings which is important, and the pattern should be clear in the initial contents list.

Once the headings are ordered, even provisionally, the material will fit more easily into place, and the more detailed the preliminary organization is, the easier the writing will be. This stage of report preparation is often rushed, the writer being understandably anxious to get down to the 'real' job of writing the report, but problems can be foreseen and so avoided if time is given to the organization. A 'jump' in the logical pattern of headings suggests that a sub-section may have been omitted and more information should be given at that point; a large number of sub-headings might suggest that too much information is being forced under one main heading; a sub-section which resolutely remains at one page and refuses to grow might more usefully be amalgamated with another sub-section; a heading which does not clearly cover the material in its sub-headings should be made more precise. Flexibility of headings and of material is essential until the writer is happy with the contents list (still provisional) and the way in which it reveals how the material is logically organized.

Notation

As the logic of the report is seen in the headings, so it is also apparent in the notation. All reports have a numbering system of some kind, whether simple:

1. Introduction

2. Findings

3. Comments

or the more complex but highly recommended decimal notation system. Numbers and headings are linked: each number will have a heading beside it to show where it fits into the report pattern. It is helpful to have a system which is widely used and easily recognized, which is one of the two great advantages of decimal notation, the other being the logic which is inherent in it. If a mixed system is used, the reader will find it difficult to decide whether (b) comes before or after (iii) and how it relates to (A). It will also be hard to identify a single section with its sub-sections, and this will be a greater problem for the report user than for the report reader. Roman numerals (i, ii, iii, etc.,) should always be avoided, as many people find them difficult to work out, and they are liable to be confused with letters.

Decimal notation avoids all these problems. The major sections are given single arabic numbers (1, 2, 3, etc.,) in sequential order, the first level of sub-section will follow a decimal point (1.1), and the first sub-section under that sub-section will repeat the process (1.1.1). It is possible to sub-divide many times, but for practical purposes four numbers is the maximum, and three will often be sufficient. The use of a string of numbers (1.1.3.4.6, etc.)

suggests that the material has not been well organized; in the course of handling very many technical reports, we have not found an example of a well-constructed report which has used more than three levels of numbers after the decimal point.

The reader will be further helped if the form of the headings agrees with the decimal hierarchy, and reinforces it. If the major number has the boldest heading (upper case, underlined, bold type as available), then the first level sub-division will have a form of heading which is clearly subordinate (initial captials, no underlining, small type size), and this reinforcement of the hierarchy can continue for as long as there are forms available to differentiate between the levels. If we look back to the report on systems of insulation, again assuming that House Insulation is the third section, we can see how the three areas mentioned, walls, loft and windows, will be organized.

3. HOUSE INSULATION
....

3.1 Walls
3.1.1 Cavity Filling
....
....

3.1.2 Dry Lining
....
....
....

3.1.3 Pebble Decking
....
....

3.2 Loft
....
....

3.2.1 Fibre Glass
....

3.2.2 Polystyrene Tiles
....
....

3.3 Windows
....
3.3.1 Double Glazing
....
....
3.3.2 Brick over
....

Some headings will have information immediately under them (as **3.2 Loft**

16

has) and some will move from major heading to subordinate heading (as 3.1 is followed at once by 3.1.1): the material available is the criterion. The advantage of this system for the report user is that if he is interested only in loft insulation, he can see at once from the contents list where his section is located, that it begins at 3.2 and that it ends at 3.3 The contents list will give at least the first two levels of heading, together with the page numbers.

In the layout shown above, each subordinate heading is indented. This is useful in short reports, but in a long report the effect can be to move all the material over to the right hand side and so to waste a great deal of paper. In such a case, the headings can be placed in line with one another:

3. HOUSE INSULATION
    ....

3.1 Walls
3.1.1 Cavity Filling
    ....

3.1.2 Dry Lining
    ....

3.1.3 Pebble Decking
    ....

and so on. However, each heading should be on a new line, and the section or sub-section under it should also start on a new line, so that the heading can be easily located. In a long report, major sections may start on a new page, possibly with their own sectional contents list under the major heading.

Occasionally, the writer may require a list of items to be included in the decimal notation system, without wanting the individual items in the list to be identified separately. A report which discussed life cycle costing in construction[3] introduced the basis for costing an individual building with a series of questions:

• Where it is located?
• Are there any drawings available?
• What is the breakdown of the functional floor areas?
• What is the general construction?
• What is its general condition?
• When was it built?

There are many more questions, all dealt with later in the report, but the introductory list is not in itself referred to. The items are therefore 'blob-bed', identified by a large black dot to the left of each item, easily seen but not requiring a level of decimal notation. If it is necessary to list items and to refer to them individually, they can be identified by arabic numbers in brackets to the left of the item. The questions listed above could have been handled in this way if it had been found necessary to comment on them, for instance:

(1) Where is it located?
(2) Are there any drawings available?
(3) What is the breakdown of the functional floor areas?

and, at the end of the list, perhaps:

Question (1) is important, as local climatic conditions affect the
materials used...

Again, the items can be identified without the need for further decimal
numbering.

In this chapter, we have stressed the value of decimal notation, as both
logical and widely used. However, other forms of notation are sometimes
found, one of them especially in Government reports. This is the numbering
of every paragraph throughout the report. It can be useful if the whole work
is short, and likely to be the subject of meetings and telephone discussions,
when the need to identify a small quantity of material quickly is imperative.
It is, on the other hand, not logical, except that paragraph 647 is found
between 646 and 648. The reader cannot tell whether paragraph 647 is more
general and introductory than 648, or whether a new major section of the
report begins at 649. It is impossible to extract a major section and know
at once that it is complete, as the reader could know that section 6.4 began
at 6.4 and ended at 6.5. A side-effect of using paragraph numbering is the
production of very long paragraphs, the writer being unwilling to create an
artificial sub-division by starting a new paragraph and so continuing the
current one for three-quarters of a page! Decimal notation, of course, allows
for several paragraphs under the same heading, if it is appropriate. With
the minor exception of the very short report discussed orally, there seems
little to recommend the paragraph style of numbering. It does not even
produce a satisfactory contents list, as headings can be listed but their relative
importance cannot be seen in the notation.

Pagination

Reference has already been made to page numbers. Surprisingly, many reports
appear, printed or typed, without page numbers, sometimes as a result of
poor photocopying (the number was on the original, but disappeared from
the top or bottom of the page in the copying) but often because nobody
thought to add the numbers. The manager assumes that the secretary will
do so, and the secretary presumes that the numbers are not there because
they are not wanted. Word processors will usually number the pages, if asked.
Pagination is not just the final job when the report is completed, but a useful
process from the stage at which a section is written, even in draft. For
instance, the writer has completed the analysis of his experimental data, and
as a result has 30 pages of handwritten or typed material. From his draft

contents list, he sees that these pages will probably form section 4 of the report. He can now number the pages as 4/1, 4/2, 4/3 and so on. If the pages are accidentally out of order when the typist receives them, the fact is obvious, and the typist himself can put the order right (an impossible task for a non-specialist in the subject if the pages are not numbered). The writer's own time may well be saved, as the authors of this book know to their cost, having had painful experience of the open window and the suddenly-opened door, and the resultant chaos of papers on the floor. If, later, the report writer wishes to add a page in the middle of his section, he simply adds page 4/15a, making a note on page 4/15 that it will be followed by 4/15a and on page 4/16 that it follows 4/15a. A similar process shows where a page has been deleted ('no 4/15'). When all the sections are completed, the page numbering can be finalized, preferably in arabic numbers throughout, at the centre top or right-hand top corner of the page.

'Throughout' is an important word in the previous sentence, as some reports have different sequences in their paging: roman numerals are often used for the preliminary pages, and a new sequence is sometimes introduced for each appendix. Pages which are entirely diagrammatic in content are occasionally omitted entirely from the numbering, with dire results. All pages which follow the title page, contents list and summary should be included in one sequence, and the page numbers will appear, of course, on the final contents list:

Contents

Section	Page
1 Principles of Insulation	1
2 Modern Insulation Techniques	15
3 House Insulation	24
3.1 Walls	25
3.2 Loft	38

Naturally, the final pagination is indeed a last minute job, especially if the report is printed.

Appendices

So far, we have considered material which is in category A only (see Chapter 2), but the pile of information in the B category (more or less relevant, or relevant to some readers if not all) has also been growing. This was considered as material for the appendix and, if the report writer has not changed his mind, that is where it will appear. Appendices are the writer's friends, allowing him to include information which is not in the mainstream of his report but which he is not willing to jettison. They are also a partial answer to the most difficult of problems, the diverse readership. They represent the last resting place of that which is borderline—relevant or of interest to the specialist only.

The terms of reference of a report may ask the writer to consider three possible ways of heating a building. In his findings, he has investigated each method, looked at its installation and maintenance costs, its efficiency, and its general suitability for the building involved. The conclusions have shown the difference between the three types, pointing out that while Type X is expensive and difficult to install, its running costs will be lower than those of Type Y, which is much easier to install. The human race being what it is, the people who work in the building are all clamouring for Type Z, which is expensive to install and to run, but which is efficient, quiet and flexible to seasonal changes of temperature. The report writer has looked at all the pros and cons and, with a sigh of relief that he is only the report writer and will not have to live with the consequences, has recommended Type X. The staff will get used to it (having little option) and it will be economical to run.

So the recommendation is Type X, for all the appropriate reasons, and the report writer is left with a mass of detailed material about the running costs of Types Y and Z. Clearly, these are not irrelevant to the report, but equally obviously, more detail will be given about Type X, with enough information to show why it will eventually be cheaper than the other two. This is a clear case for the use of appendices. The detailed examples of the method and the cost of using Types Y and Z will become Appendix A and Appendix B (it is useful to give appendices letters rather than numbers, to keep them separate from the main part of the report). When, after many meetings and much lengthy discussion, the general manager decides on Type Z (after all, he has to work with the company employees every day and to put up with their complaints), he will have the information he needs available at the end of the report. If, two years later, anyone complains about the cost of the new heating system, all the evidence is available to show what a dreadful mistake was made, and while this may be unfortunate for the general manager, the report writer is exonerated.

The general manager may decide to move on, and some years later his successor will be faced with the rising cost of heating the building and will wonder why on earth such a crazy decision was made in the first place. The report will provide him with the evidence, if not the answer to his problem, and this is another aspect of the usefulness of appendices. They provide the back-up information which is invaluable to those who follow the original decision-makers, and ensure that, with luck, the same mistakes are not made again.

Appendices are also of use to the specialist reader. Our old friend the insulation report is a useful example. The main material of the report deals with the insulation of public buildings, libraries and town halls, and, in Section 3, with the insulation of houses. The report user reads Section 3, and is dubious. It all makes sense in theory, but what about his limited budget? He wants some worked examples which include his ordinary three-bedroomed house and which show what percentage of warmth he will keep

20

if he can afford to insulate one area only. There in the appendices are his examples, and he discovers with interest that double glazing, although useful, will not save him as much in heating costs as will loft insulation. In the same way, experimental data which are of interest only to the expert reader can usefully be presented in an appendix, as can supporting statistics, or maps and charts (but for a more detailed discussion of the position of diagrammatic material, see Chapter 5). The main text remains uncluttered with detail not needed by most readers, while that detail is available for the few readers who will need it.

If it is necessary to sub-divide an appendix, the sections can follow a decimal notation pattern preceded by the appendix letter. So B3.1 is the first sub-division of the third section of Appendix B. Needless to say, so much detailed division is rarely necessary. The appendices are, nevertheless, an integral part of the report, listed in the contents and included in the page numbering.

Review of headings

Once the main text plan is established and the order of appendices decided, much of the preparatory work is done. By this time, some small factual sections of the report are written, and the whole structure is becoming clear and logically expressed. Headings must be checked for accuracy and for precision, and again the contents list is useful. The report writer should go back to the contents and ask himself what he would expect to find under each of the headings. 'Services' might have been a useful starting place, but if he came new to the report and saw the heading, what would he expect? Bus, train, church, tennis, after-sales, gas and electricity, or the army, navy and air force? The word is much too wide in its implications to be used as a heading without further definition. The length and complexity of sections should also be again revised: are more—or fewer—sub-divisions needed? The organization of the report must be revised regularly until the clearest, most precise and helpful headings are found, and the logic of the whole made obvious and accessible to the reader.

A further word is needed on the subject of headings and, indeed, report titles. Precision is crucially important, for the sake of the report writer as well as the reader, for a vague title probably means that the report will be overlooked, and it is disheartening to spend time and effort only to find one's work neglected. As a rule, it is better to have a short title than a long one: it is more easily remembered, it attracts the attention more readily, and it is easier to identify, especially if a company's reports are filed by keywords on the computer. Sometimes, however, a title will have to be lengthy simply because to shorten it would be to change its meaning or its scope. A useful compromise can be a very short title followed by a longer, more explanatory sub-title, as in the Cockcroft Report (HMSO, 1982):

Mathematics Counts
Report of the Committee of Inquiry into the teaching of
mathematics in schools.

The short title succeeds in attracting attention, while the longer sub-title gives precise information about the subject of the report. As with most writing, the author must sit back and look at the title and the headings as dispassionately as possible. Questions as headings tend to downgrade a report to the level of leaflets which fall on the doormat, asking 'Why not double glaze your windows?' to which there is either no reply because talking to a leaflet seems ridiculous or a useless reply such as 'Because I've done so already!' This is not as far-fetched an analogy as it sounds, since asking questions in a report heading has just the same effect: there is no way the reader can answer, and in any case he is reading the report precisely because he is interested in the subject and will ask the questions himself. There is also the problem of unintentional humour:

The growth of timber framed houses

is a good title in principle, but suggests inevitably that little timber framed houses grow into bigger timber framed houses, which might be useful for their owners. An analysis of the different sections of a particular company's internal communications network ended up with the following heading:

The breakdown of the telephone system

thus giving rise to suggestions of trouble where there was none. Clearly, titles need serious consideration by report writers.

Conclusions and recommendations

The organization of the main findings of the report will follow the pattern suggested above, with its appropriate headings and notation. The conclusions are there to bring together material which, although scattered through the findings, can be identified as presenting a common aspect which sums up much that has gone before: on the basis of the evidence, the writer concludes that certain problems have been identified. In his recommendations, he will (if asked) suggest ways of solving the problems, possibly stressing one or more particularly important or urgent solutions. Both conclusions and recommendations continue the headings and notation pattern of the earlier part of the report, and the writer must be sure that no new evidence which was not revealed in the findings appears at this late stage. The evidence must, in the main body of the text, precede the conclusions.

Recommendations are not always asked for in the terms of reference, and many reports end with the conclusions. Sometimes in-company or inter-company politics mean that recommendations have to be hinted at rather than stated clearly, and as usual the policy of the writer's organization is binding on the writer. However, where both conclusions and recommendations appear, they must be kept separate. In principle, the conclusions are an objective assessment of the facts, while the recommendations are the writer's subjective view of how the facts should be dealt with, but in practice the subjective/objective distinction is blurred. In selecting some facts and rejecting others, in considering the evidence, the writer is inevitably subjective. Nevertheless, the recommendations are the writer's ideas and he is responsible for their implications, which is, indeed, one of the principal reasons for the signing and dating of all reports. The writer accepts his responsibility, and often his superior in the organization will in turn accept responsibility by adding his signature as ratification of what has been produced and sometimes also to signify permission for the document to be released.

A simple example will illustrate the distinction between the conclusions and the recommendations. In an old office building, there is a rather steep staircase with an awkward turn in it. One winter afternoon, a secretary, carrying a large pile of papers, falls on the stairs and breaks his arm. An accident report form is completed, but the office manager feels that further investigation is needed, and asks a member of the personnel staff to have a closer look at the circumstances in which the incident took place. It becomes clear that there have been a number of minor complaints about the difficulty of negotiating the staircase, especially in poor light, comments that the stair carpet is becoming worn in places (although not yet dangerous in itself), and a general feeling that the secretary was negligent in knowing of the hazard and yet trying to carry so large an amount of paper that his view of the staircase was impaired. The conclusions of the report were therefore that:

1. the staircase was awkward when natural light was not good;

2. the state of the carpet did not contribute to the accident, but it was worn in places;

3. the accident was caused in part by the amount of paper being carried at the time;

4. previous complaints about the staircase had not resulted in action.

These are conclusions based on investigation and, probably, interview. They are objective facts, and do not in themselves suggest action to be taken: they follow from the evidence presented.

When the writer turns to the recommendations, he has to assess what should be done on the basis of his conclusions. The light on the staircase is obviously a problem, and extra light fittings with stronger bulbs or fluorescent strips might be recommended. A potential hazard in the form of the carpet has been revealed, and the writer might well suggest *at this point in the report* that the carpet should be replaced and that in choosing the colour, the problem of visibility should be taken into account. Such a suggestion is the writer's own, based on his conclusions but in no way hinted at within the conclusions section. How much he chooses to recommend about his third and fourth conclusions will depend on his overall view of the situation: do staff normally carry quantities of paper down the stairs, and if so, should they be warned to be careful, and is there a wider implication that reasonable complaints by the staff are ignored by those responsible for health and safety at work? Further recommendations may be called for, or, on the other hand, it may be assumed that the incident is unlikely to be repeated and that the reasonable channels for complaint had been ignored by the staff, in spite of general awareness that the channels existed. Obviously, this is a simplistic example, as such an incident would in reality involve, for example, the union safety representative, but the pattern in clear: conclusions are a consideration of the evidence while recommendations suggest action as a result of such consideration, and they are normally kept apart.

References and bibliography

By the time that the report writer has completed his introduction, findings, conclusions and recommendations, and organized the appendices of the report, most of the work is done. There remain a few aspects of the format of the report which still need consideration, and one of these will have been kept in mind since the report was begun. Many reports have neither references nor a bibliography, but some have either or both, and the preparation of these sections will continue throughout the organization and writing of the rest of the report. References show the published (or occasionally non-published) work which has been used in the writing, quoted from and specifically mentioned, and there are accepted ways of showing both the textual mark and the full details of the sources. A bibliography is a list of published work (again, occasionally non-published, for instance a thesis) which has not been specifically referred to in the text, but which will be of interest and use to the reader. If both are included in a report, they must be in separate lists, the references first, usually in the order in which they occur in the text, and then the bibliography, usually in alphabetical order of author or body responsible for the production of the item.

A reference, once forgotten, is difficult to recall. As soon as it is apparent that books, journals, other reports and similar material will be used or mentioned in the text, the writer should start to prepare the lists which will form the bases of the bibliographical sections. The easiest way to do this is to have two sets of file cards, and to record all relevant information on a card, as soon as it is found. The card is then filed under 'references' if the source will be mentioned in the text, and under 'bibliography' if it is of general interest but not specifically mentioned or quoted from. The reverse side of the card can be used for comments, either about the quality and usefulness of the reference, or about where it came from (library or similar), or, of course, both. All the details recorded must be correct, and it is always wise in the writing of the report to record all useful material: it is much easier to reject a card later than to hunt for missing information. Report writers are normally responsible for checking the copyright position of material quoted, and if necessary obtaining written permission to quote. As a reference is recorded, the text should be marked to remind the writer to complete the textual mark when it is possible to do so, as the order in which the references are found will probably not be the final order in which they are listed.

Most references come from one or more of five kinds of source:

books
journals
published reports
conference proceedings
reports produced by the writer's own company

There are various kinds of textual mark possible, of which the most widely used is probably the superscript arabic number, as in the following example:

A study published recently[4] shows that current research...

However, in the case of reports with a high percentage of mathematical content, it is often sensible to use a superscript number with an upturned bracket, to avoid confusion with equations or formulae:

A study published recently[4] shows that current research...

If the upturned bracket is not available, square brackets are a sensible substitute (not superscript as a rule):

A study published recently [4] shows that current research...

Any of these forms is possible, but company policy may dictate a particular form, as may the nature of the report material. Consistency is essential, whichever form is chosen.

Consistency is also necessary in the full form of the reference at the end of the report. (References are occasionally placed at the foot of the appropriate page, but footnotes are difficult to type and expensive for a printer to set, and should be avoided if possible.) Common forms of references are given below, but if a different form is chosen, the writer must be careful to include all important information, and to be consistent in the layout. Usually the references will be in the order in which they occur in the report, and the numbers will therefore be sequential. The examples given are, clearly, fictitious!

Example 1   Book Reference
14   Bloggs, J., *Electronics for All*, McGraw-Hill, 15th edn, 1994.

Example 2   Journal Reference
19   Bloggs, J., 'Electronics for the undergraduate', *Electronic World*, **88**, August 1992, pp. 16-29.

Example 3   Report Reference
96   Bloggs, Judith, *Working in electronics*, April 1990, National Engineering Laboratory, NEL Report no. 999.

Example 4   Conference Proceedings Reference
102   Bloggs, James, 'Communication courses for engineers,' in *The Education of an Engineer*, Conference Proceedings, Reading College of Technology, 1 April 1999, pp. 222-233.

In the case of reference to reports produced by the writer's own company, the organization's standard policy should be followed; if the report is published, the publishers will give guidance about the correct form of reference. As a general rule, the words underlined or in italics will be those which appear on the spine of a published book.

It is always sensible to give as much information as possible, including the most complete form of the author's name. Various members of a family may publish books on related subjects (as indicated by the fictitious Bloggs family), and the particular author should be identified. If there are two authors, both names will be given:

21   Bloggs, Judith and Amanda Bloggs, *The Growth of the Electronics Industry: a Historic Survey*, McGraw-Hill, 2nd edn, 1996.

However, if there are more than two authors, it is customary to give the first only, indicating that others exist:

46   Bloggs, J., *et al.*, *Electronics in the Twenty-first Century*, McGraw-Hill, 1998.

The date is essential in all references: books go out of date quickly, especially in the field of technology, and the reader will judge the value of the report partly by the dates of the references (and by the edition number, particularly when a book has rapidly run to several editions). References must always be checked, as few things are more frustrating to a reader than to hunt for a reference and be unable to find it, perhaps for as simple a reason as transposed page numbers. Above all, the writer should give accurate information, and be consistent in his chosen format.

Much of what has been said about references applies also to the bibliography. The information should be as full as possible and consistent, but the items are usually listed in alphabetical order of author, the details being given in the forms suggested in the examples above. There are, of course, no textual marks as the works listed have not been specifically mentioned in the text.

The summary

There remains in the writing of a report the report writer's nightmare, the summary. This has to be the final section written, and in some ways it is the most difficult. In a small space (perhaps 10 or 12 lines of type, for a report of 50 or 60 pages), the author has to give a miniaturized picture of the report not only for the report reader, but also for those who will never set eyes on the whole report. The summary has grown in importance in recent years. Originally, it was intended as an introduction to the report, giving the reader an overall view, and it still serves this purpose. It is also a reminder of the essentials of the report for the reader who has read the whole work but who needs to have his memory refreshed, perhaps before going to a meeting at which the subject of the report is discussed. It is a helpful overall picture, too, for the report user, showing how his section fits into the report as a whole. However, the summary has another, and more delicate, task. It will probably take on a life of its own, independent of the rest of the report, and be circulated to a number of people who have a general interest in the subject but who have neither time nor inclination to read the report. (These include people who feel that their status demands that they have a general interest in the subject, even if they haven't, or who feel that they need to have an overall view of what is going on in the company.) For this reason, the summary is not usually included in the pagination of the report, although it will appear in the contents: a copy of the summary or summaries must be bound into the report, even if its real service is as a separate entity.

The summary page usually includes the report title, with or without reference number, and the date, with any other code which will identify the whole report or show its confidentiality. Otherwise, the summary should stand alone. It will give the reader a clear and balanced view of what the report is about, and will stress the most important or most urgent aspects of the conclusions and/or recommendations. While it gives a balanced view of the report, it is not a balanced representation of the whole, and in this it differs from a précis, which reproduces all the major thoughts of the original passage with the same stress that they had in the original. The report summary has to explain enough of the background to be intelligible to the reader who will not see the whole thing, but its greatest value is in bringing to the reader's attention that which he most needs to know, that is, what has been concluded or recommended in the light of the evidence in the report.

The report writer, then, might usefully begin preparation of the summary by sitting back and considering what are the most important aspects of his report, that is, what aspects, if he were unfortunate enough to see his report combust spontaneously, he would most want to save. He will next try to write these essentials in a few sentences, emphasizing what action must be taken as a matter of urgency. At this stage, it might be helpful to list the points to be included, numbering them as far as possible in order of priority. He then has to consider the reader's point of view. If the reader has no access to the whole report, what will he need to know in order to understand the context of these few important sentences? This information must also be written briefly, although it is better to include too much material than not enough. As with précis writing, it is much easier to cut a passage which is too long than to add to a passage which is too short. These two sections, the background and the essential recommendations, have next to be knitted together to read as a whole piece of prose, with 'link words' (see Chapter 4) to guide the reader. There is, however, no need to keep the final summary in one paragraph (again, unlike a précis); if two or three short paragraphs are more helpful than one long one, then divide up the writing.

If the preparation of the summary has been well done, the result will be unambiguous and accurate, but too long. Now the writer can look for the wordy expression ('in the first instance' is the same as but longer than 'firstly'), cut out repetition, and omit any detail which, on reflection, he feels is not essential. This is probably a good time at which to call on a colleague and ask him to read the summary to see if it makes sense or if some necessary information has been left out. It is clear by now that the writing of the summary cannot be left for the last ten minutes: it is a complicated piece of work, and, as it is the first section of the report to be read, it must be impressive.

Earlier in this chapter an example was given of conclusions and recommendations, in a report on the investigation of the circumstances and site of an accident on an office staircase. We can use the same information as an example of how the report summary would be written. The writer would mention the accident (but without details), and the place where it happened. Since he is not reporting on the accident itself, the time and the poor natural light would not be important, and although the apparent neglect of complaints made is in itself important, the recommendations would show whether it had proved worthy of further investigation. Most of the summary would therefore deal with the need to improve the lighting and to replace worn carpeting before it became a hazard. If the writer had concluded that more safety notices were needed, or that there should be better communication of potential dangers between staff and management, then these points would also appear in the summary. The need for urgent action might also be stressed. So the summary would clarify the need for the investigation, but principally would show (perhaps for the benefit of other departments in other parts of the building) what recommendations had been made.

Title page

There remains the title page, which may not be the responsibility of the author, if his company uses a standard format. However, if the author has a say in the matter, he should beware the overcrowded title page. A good layout is important, for the first impression the report makes is by its appearance, on the shelf or desk (when the binding will, or will fail to, impress) and when it is opened and the reader looks at the first page. Some information is essential: the title, the name of the author or group responsible for the production of the report, and the date. Other information will appear because of the organization to which the writer belongs: the company name, perhaps the logo and address, a reference number by which the report is identified, and sometimes also the signature of the senior manager responsible for the approval and distribution of the report. Apart from any classification such as 'Confidential', there should be nothing more on the title page, as a crowded page looks untidy and tends to distract from what the reader is most likely to read, the author and title of the report. Distribution lists are better kept on a separate sheet or, if necessary, added on the verso of the title page. Placing the summary on the title page, which is occasionally done in order to save paper, is not recommended.

Two of the items mentioned in the previous paragraph need emphasis. The author of a report (or his organization) must decide on the date to be put on the title page: it might be the date on which the first draft is completed, or on which the report goes to the typist, or on which it is completed as a document (this being the most likely), or that on which it is approved. Whichever date is chosen, that date must appear on the report, and most suitably on the title page. The presence of the date is to some extent a safety net for the writer. He is responsible for the contents of the report on that date, but if subsequent legal or financial or other changes invalidate what he has recommended, then (assuming that he could not have foreseen such an eventuality) he is not responsible for what has happened after that date. An undated report can be a time-bomb for its author. The date is also necessary for future readers. The authors of this book have seen test reports on machinery which could kill or seriously injure its operator, and the reports have been undated. It is surely essential for the operators to know whether the tests are recent, or 10 years out of date and possibly invalidated by more recent research. A report without a date should never be allowed to pass from writer to reader, whether inside or outside the writer's company.

Problems are also sometimes caused by the classification of documents. Terms such as 'Confidential' should be used only when they are strictly necessary, or they are degraded in impact. If they are used, they should be used in such a way that the classification is immediately obvious, that is, on the cover if possible, and certainly on the title page and on all pages of text. It is too easy to use the word once, often in the top left-hand corner of the title page where it can be overlooked, and forget that in the nature of reports, the user may not look at the beginning first. In the case of restricted reports, the copy number may be needed (Copy 3 of 6, for example), and if an organization has its own code to show the restriction of a report, that code should always be adhered to, and should always be apparent on the report itself.

Binding

The binding of a report is perhaps not strictly part of the format, but most companies have a policy, more or less followed, about the bindings to be used for different sorts of report. Expensive and impressive reports will sometimes go to a designer (wisely, as a typographer, for instance, will make the best impact with the report material), and will be professionally bound. Spiral bindings are often favoured for smaller reports, and they have the advantage of allowing the pages to open flat, which is particularly useful if there are many diagrams. Slide bar binding is common for internal reports: it is cheap and looks satisfactory, but it often makes opening the report difficult and can be irritating in use. Ring binders are bulky, but in many ways more satisfactory. Companies often have a company colour which is used for all external reports, and sometimes a different colour for internal reports. Whatever cover is used, it should be easy for the reader to use, should hold the pages firmly in place so that none gets lost, and should look attractive.

Text, binding and cover combine to interest the reader and to hold his attention. They should therefore be considered together, as the results of producing the text without reference to the binding can be disastrous, with holes punched through essential numbers, and the beginnings of words disappearing into the binding. The commonly-used plastic cover with a 'window' through which the title of the report and its author's name appear is sensible and reasonable in price, but the typist must be given a blank cover to use as a guide. The reader may be irritated to see the report title and 'by', with the author's name hidden by the cover, but for once the goodwill of the author is also worth considering. Years of work spent writing reports without the gratification of seeing one's name in print does nothing for the writer's confidence.

In all that has been written in this chapter about the format of reports, it is obvious that the reader's convenience is the paramount consideration, as it is also in the writing and in the diagrammatic presentation. Flexibility is therefore necessary, and company policy, usually the overriding force, should allow for some variation in style, layout and organization if the result will be an increase of goodwill. Failure to consider the total impact can result in lack of credibility, as the following real-life comment on a tender document shows:

The fact that (the company's) later submissions were presented in a very muddled form does not inspire confidence in this contractor.

CHAPTER 4

Words, words

'Words, words, words,' commented Hamlet, thus expressing the despair of many report writers and incidentally also their habit of saying the same thing three times. Words undoubtedly cause difficulties, not least by taking on a life of their own and being understood in different ways by different readers.

Hamlet and his creator had a way with words, using them not only fluently but also beautifully. Reports are not, generally speaking, read for their literary qualities, but they must be unambiguous, grammatically correct and as easy as possible to read. In this last respect, Shakespeare and the average report writer have one thing in common: the craft of writing. Contrary to popular belief, good writing is not merely a gift of nature, although it is undoubtedly easier for some people than for others. It is also a craft, and a good writer, whether of plays or reports, will work at his writing, revising, changing, worrying at a sentence or a paragraph until it is as well written as possible, which means as readable as possible.

The usual objection to this is that time gets in the way of good writing, and even of accurate writing. If the report has to go off to Riyadh by courier at the end of the afternoon, the writer cannot spend time polishing up his style, however desirable that might be. This is, of course, a valid objection, but a writer who is aware of the requirements of good style and the pitfalls of bad, will think about the art of writing when he does have time, when he is writing a report for the Parent/Teacher Association, or a letter to his local paper about traffic congestion; he will also notice when he reads something which is well written. The technical skills will be practised whenever possible, noticed whenever the opportunity arises, and will gradually become a habit. It will then become apparent that a well written report creates goodwill in the reader, does not create lawsuits because it was ambiguous, and generally brings credit to the writer's company. Good writing, in fact, has become good management and cost effective, too.

However, Hamlet's habit of repetition resulted from dramatic and psychological necessity: the report writer's from lack of confidence. If the writer is not sure of the reader's comprehension, he might consider repeating the idea in different words. Indeed, if the writer becomes carried away by this technique, the same idea could be repeated again and again, which wastes writer's, reader's and typist's time. If the idea is expressed precisely and concisely at the first writing, everyone is happy.

This chapter, then, will look first at the problems which words cause, and will suggest ways of controlling them so that they are not masters but servants, and the most obedient servants at that.

Spelling

A word has first of all to be recognized: for example, 'eleviate' is a combination of 'elevate' and 'alleviate', and it is not necessarily clear which is meant. Bad spelling not only gives a poor impression but also creates confusion. For some inexplicable reason, the world is divided into two categories: those who can spell without difficulty, and those who can't. There seems to be no justice in the distribution, and little heredity either. We all know examples of a brother and sister, one of whom can spell correctly and the other of whom has great difficulty in remembering how many 'l's there are at the end of 'until'. Many good, fluent, intelligent writers have spelling problems, and the English language does little to help them.

Rules, as will be seen later in this chapter, help with punctuation, but are little help with spelling. A few, such as 'i before e except after c, as long as the sound is ee' work some of the time, but most rules are based on complex stress patterns or on the original Latin or Greek words from which the English words are derived, or have so many exceptions that the rule is hardly worth the effort needed to learn it.

There is, however, some hope for the world's poor spellers, even though it is hope founded on hard work. In order to attack the problem, the report writer needs to see words in three categories, which must be treated in different ways.

First, there are complex technical words which only the regular user could hope to spell correctly. These do not often cause trouble, as they clearly have to be learnt, and the typist should have a technical dictionary and a list of specific, frequently-occurring words to refer to. Occasionally, words which are not technical but which are common in the writer's profession are mis-spelt because they have never been checked: a surprising number of engineers cannot spell 'maintenance', of mechanics cannot spell 'vehicle', and of managers cannot spell 'committee'. These words are not strictly in the first category, but it is as well not to take for granted the standard words of one's trade until they have been checked with the dictionary.

Second, there is the enormous number of words which are clearly out to get the writer. These gremlin words are notorious, 'necessary' probably being the best-known; others include 'separate', 'definite', 'liaison', 'correspondence' and 'procedure'. If the reader can honestly say that he would make no mistake with such words, he is a born 'good speller', and should appreciate his good fortune. If many such words cause problems, then the reader does not share this good fortune, and will have to work hard. However, there is only a limited number of common words with traps in them, and from that the poor speller may take comfort. If these words are learnt, a few at a time, spelling mistakes will be considerably reduced. For unusual words, a dictionary should always be referred to, even by good spellers: guessing is not the answer.

Third, there are words which inhabit a grey area between right and wrong. Some such words are new to the language, which has not yet decided how to deal with them: 'data base' may be written as two separate words, or hyphenated; 'word processor' is seen as two words or as one, or even occasionally with a hyphen. In time these words will cease to give trouble, and in the meantime it is best to select what seems to be the most commonly found form and then to be consistent.

Hyphens are used much less frequently than in the past. 'Today' was once written 'to-day', which now seems strange, and on the whole we use hyphens only to join words which would otherwise be ambiguous: 'extra-rational' is *outside* reason; 'extra rational' might mean 'more reasonable than usual'. Sometimes the distinction of meaning is most important: 'a cross-section of staff' is quite different from 'a cross section of staff', and 'a crosssection of staff' looks silly (English dislikes to see the same letter written consecutively three times: hence 'Mrs Jones's shop' is more commonly written as 'Mrs Jones' shop').

Divergences between English and American usage have also to be remembered. Generally, each country understands that the other has words which are spelt in a different way, such as the American single 'l' in a word like 'traveling', or 'color' instead of the English 'colour'. Unless there is a request for a particular version, it is simplest to keep to the forms with which the writer is most familiar. A few words are probably in transition and some do not fit happily to English usage, as the American addition of 'wise' as a suffix ('pricewise'); 'alright' may be acceptable in the United States, but only 'all right' is correct in England. No doubt other words will cross the Atlantic, or sink in mid-ocean, in the future. It is helpful if a typist whose reports may travel outside the United Kingdom has both an English and an American dictionary available, to use as company policy dictates.

Gremlin words often come in pairs, linked by their sound or by their appearance. 'Principle' and 'principal' sound very similar but have different meanings (principles are to do with morality; the principal is the boss), while 'deprecate' and 'depreciate' are lookalikes, but should not be confused (to deprecate is to deplore something, while depreciate is what secondhand cars do). Some pairs have similar derivations but have moved far apart: 'uninterested' simply means having no interest in, while 'disinterested' means impartial. A magistrate may safely be the latter, but never the former, which suggests boredom. Words occasionally change spelling when they are used for different parts of speech: we may advise a course of action but we give advice, and a licence to kill does not mean that we are necessarily licensed to do so. Nor should we devise a murderous device.

Choice of words

Some words mean too little and others too much. 'Empty' words are frequently used to occupy space without the need for thought: 'quite satisfactory' is not noticeably different from 'satisfactory', and 'absolutely fatal' suggests degrees of death in the same way that 'totally complete' suggests that some things are more complete than others. The effect of using 'quite', 'fairly', 'rather' and other such empty words is to suggest that the writer lacks confidence in his material, which should never be true of report writers.

On the other hand, a common affliction is the desire to impress by using inflated language, words which are too big for their context. 'Pay' and 'remuneration' do not always mean the same thing, but if pay is what we are receiving, we should be grateful and not demand a more impressive name for it. 'Advise' meaning 'tell' or 'inform' should be kept distinct from 'advise' meaning 'give advice', and a 'locality' is no more than a 'place'. Sometimes whole phrases mean the same as a single word: 'we are in a position to undertake' probably means 'we can'. It is always a temptation to describe a problem as a crisis, but if we do, there is no word left for the crisis when it happens. The pompously written sentence:

Inspection of the kitchen suggests that many items of equipment are left on when not in use and this mode of operation should be avoided

is easily ignored: a large 'SWITCH OFF' notice above the cooker has immediate impact.

Words and phrases can lose their meaning with over-use. The most famous cliché, 'Unaccustomed as I am to public speaking', could now be used only for humorous effect and not out of humility. Letters which begin 'I am writing to inform you' state the obvious, while 'in this day and age' certainly 'leaves much to be desired' and should be 'conspicuous by its absence'. Closely related to the cliché is unnecessary jargon. Necessary jargon is the tool of the trade (cliché) that is, professionally used words which are acceptable to readers from the same profession, who will clearly understand the meaning. 'Geotechnics' is a pleasant word used by geologists, while most of us would probably settle for 'geological features' or some such part-equivalent; a Cartomancy Congress sounds highly scientific, but would a Fortune Tellers' Congress have the same effect? If, and the 'if' is important, the reader understands and uses the same term, then it is acceptable jargon. However, unnecessary jargon is highly infectious and much less desirable. 'Basically' is a good word if the writer means 'this is the basis of what I am writing about', but its popularity as a sentence filler is to be deplored. A 'facilitator' helps a 'situation', which sounds fine but means little. Indeed, the spread of unnecessary jargon is such that sentences can be created of 90 per cent meaninglessness:

At this present moment in time, we are experiencing an ongoing crisis situation with our *Brassica oleracea*, although in due course a substantial number will become viable and at the end of the day they will be readily available at the neighbourhood retailing outlet.

In other words, 'We've a shortage of cabbages now, but they will be in the shops soon'. ('Substantial' is a 'loaded' word: you might see my wage rise as substantial, but I probably wouldn't; it's almost as bad as 'up to 30% off', meaning 'only 1% off, but we wish it could have been 29%'!)

'Loaded' words have meanings which are sensed by the reader, as well as intellectually understood dictionary meanings. To be interviewed can be pleasurably exciting (a new job, promotion), but to be questioned suggests trouble with the police. We may attempt to make a point forcefully, but sound aggressive to others. A crowd is described as a mob, and there has clearly been trouble. The choice of one word rather than another suggests overtones of meaning to the reader, and the choice has to be made with subtle skill (or deviousness, depending how you look at it) in order to make sure that the effect is the one desired. As is so often true in using English, awareness is the key. The more we notice words and how other people use them, the more we become responsive to the power of words and the more skilful our own usage will become.

One final word about words. As technology advances, old words are used in new ways (*data*, a plural word, has become the equivalent of a singular collective noun), new words are invented (*breathalysers* joined the English language in about 1960), and established words take on new, additional meanings and variant spellings (*disc*, *disk*, 'flat circular plate such as a coin', is also a gramophone record or a computer storage device).

While changes are inevitable in any living language, the development of 'pseudo-words' is disturbing to the reader and does nothing to increase comprehension. Words may be joined together to form a hybrid which is not helpful: are 'socio-economic considerations' the same as 'social and economic', or is the social aspect subordinate to the economic, or, indeed, vice versa? Other 'pseudo-words' develop within particular industries. The construction industry has learnt to live with 'buildability', but 'construc-tionability' is ugly and unnecessary. We may converse by telephone more simply than 'telephonically'. 'Skeletonize' allows scope for the imagination: perhaps 'skeletonization' is the opposite of 'survivability'.

The previous paragraph is not a joke. All the words given have appeared in technical reports, and no doubt there are many others. They have no historical, literary or musical virtues, and, what is more, they make the reader laugh, or perhaps despair.

Sentences

Words do not only try to trap the writer in an individual capacity. They join together and swarm like locusts, terrifying the beholder and causing devastation and barrenness of meaning. Short sentences are easily controlled. Other sentences, containing more detailed information and being more complex in form, make greater demands on writer and reader alike. It has been known, however, for words to join together in large numbers, describing, qualifying and modifying one another, linked by words of humbler nature to form phrases and clauses of greater or lesser complexity which in turn are joined, in the nature of the sentence itself, in order to form a whole which is satisfying and intelligible to the reader.

The reader of this book will have just seen that while short sentences are easy to understand, enormous sentences are extremely difficult. If the report writer wishes to help his reader, the length of his sentences must be tightly controlled, and the purpose of each sentence established.

A series of very short sentences, of perhaps fewer than ten words, is jerky and awkward, sounding like a small child's learn-to-read book. In a report this can be useful, as a series of facts will be easily assimilated as a list composed of short sentences. As the sentence grows in length, so the rate of reading will be slowed down and the reader forced to reflect on the ideas presented. An 'average' sentence has about 17 to 20 words; if the intention is to help the reader to consider and evaluate various possible interpretations of data, sentences of 20 to 25 words will have the right effect. As soon as a sentence exceeds 30 words, there is a danger that the reader will have too much to assimilate without the breathing space of a full stop. Obviously, the complexity or otherwise of the material will affect the length of the sentences, but variety helps the flow of the reading and improves the style. Some long, some middle-sized and some short sentences produce the most readable material, but no sentence should be too long, or allowed to get out of control.

The problem of sentence control is best seen in examples, taken from real-life reports, of how words can escape from the writer's head to create confusion. A sentence must make complete sense within itself. The following is not a sentence:

> To ensure the system will not be adversely affected by periods of bad weather, or sudden failure in the mains supply, when good communications during these sometimes chaotic conditions will be essential.

To ensure the system works—what must be done? The sentence has no grammatical end, and cannot therefore make sense. We may guess at what the writer intended: the system must perform satisfactorily even under extreme conditions. How this is to be ensured, we are not told. Many sentences simply contain too much information:

> Predominantly a peak heating system such as ceiling heating which is designed for continuous operation throughout the heating season, is generally used by tenants intermittently, this gives rise to complaints of cold feet and legs, high running cost and poor value for money.

Apart from the unintentional humour of the juxtaposition of cold feet and legs and high running cost, and some grammatical oddities such as 'system' when the plural 'systems' must be intended, there is one basic problem. The sentence is too long. Its perpetrator might usefully have sat back and looked at the separate pieces of information available.

1. Ceiling heating is a form of peak heating system.

2. Any peak heating system is designed to be used continuously.

3. The limits to continuous use are decided by the weather (or the calendar, or the landlord).

4. Generally, tenants use the system intermittently.

5. The tenants(?) complain of cold feet and legs.

6. The running cost is high.

7. The system appears to be poor value for money.

There are four sections of information here. First is the explanation of the system and its intended use, second is the way in which it is nevertheless being used, third is the result of that usage from the tenants' point of view, and fourth is the economic factor. These sections immediately suggest sentences, each being a clearly defined package of information which will make complete sense in itself. So:

1. Ceiling heating, like any peak heating system, is intended to be used continuously during the period October to May (or during the winter).

2. Tenants are at present using the system intermittently.

3. As a result, the tenants complain of the apparent inefficiency of the system. They suffer from cold feet and legs.

4. The running cost of using the system in this way is high, and the landlord and the tenants are getting poor value for money.

Four sentences will make a tidy paragraph (see next section). If the report is written for the tenants, sentence 3 might be used first, while if it is written for the landlord, sentence 4 will attract immediate attention. So:

As the ceiling heating is operated at present, the running cost is high and the system appears to be poor value for money. However, as with all peak heating systems, it was designed for continuous operation throughout the winter. At present, it is used intermittently by the tenants and is therefore working inefficiently. As a result, we are receiving complaints from the tenants about cold feet and legs.

The ordering of ideas is now clear, and the paragraph is much easier to read than the original. Nevertheless, the equal length of the sentences makes for a certain monotony, and the paragraph might be improved with a little variety:

As the ceiling heating is operated at present, the running cost is high and the system appears to represent poor value for money. However, as with all peak heating systems, it was designed for continuous operation during the winter, but tenants often use it intermittently. Inevitably, they complain of the cold.

While admittedly a certain licence has been taken with the material of the original attempt, the picture is clear: wrong use of system, unhappy tenants, waste of money.

The process of sentence construction has now been analysed. First of all, the writer must decide exactly what has to be said, and, at least mentally, list the various points. Each point can be seen as a separate sentence, and the sentences arranged logically, or according to the impact on the reader. Then the sentences can be written in order, but adapted to give variety of length and structure. The process is not as lengthy as it sounds, and in any case it must be faster and cheaper than a series of letters or telephone calls needed in order to extract meaning from confused writing.

It is often helpful to read a long sentence out loud. If the report writer runs out of breath before the end, the sentence is probably too long. Where the voice pauses naturally, a comma is usually appropriate, and if the writer himself is confused at the end, then the recipients of the report certainly will be. The awkwardness of the following real-life sentence is clear as soon as it is heard:

Further investigation such as taking core samples to ascertain thickness and the degree of corosion (*sic*) of the brick mortar jointing, might be necessary to have carried out.

The next step for the report writer is to ask himself what he would say if he were confronted by the recipient. It would probably be something like this:

Well, we might have to look further, you know, perhaps take some core samples. We'd want to know about the brick mortar jointing, how thick it is, and how far it's corroded.

The original sentence is now two sentences, and the language has been simplified. It has become too chatty for a formal report, and so a balance must be found:

It might be necessary to take core samples (this stage *is* 'further investigation') to find the thickness and degree of corrosion of the brick mortar jointing.

38

Twenty-seven words have been reduced to 21, and the sentence says what it means in a straightforward way. 'Back to front' sentences are particularly irritating, as the reader has to get to the end to understand the message:

> Based on the fact that the terms and conditions of the Original Order prevail on the Amendments then these items do not fall into the Liquidated Damages period.

The writer of the sentence probably wanted to impress (hence the number of capital letters), but the second part of the sentence carries the essentials, and it should be moved to the start:

> These items do not fall into the Liquidated Damages period since the terms and conditions of the Original Order prevail over the Amendments.

Punctuation

Much of the difficulty of sentence construction comes, as has been seen, from a lack of punctuation, or from inaccurate punctuation. A good rule-of-thumb guide is to read aloud, as a full stop is intended to allow the reader time to assimilate what has gone before and prepare for what is to come, while a comma is a pause for (mental) breath. Commas also show how the sentence should be read:

1. However difficulties might arise, we will be able to solve them.

2. However difficulties might arise, although we will be able to solve them.

3. However, difficulties might arise although we will be able to solve them.

Sentences 1 and 3 are clear, and the reader knows how to understand them; Sentence 2 is not clear, because the reader cannot guess until he reaches 'although', halfway through the sentence, whether 'however' is a comment on the situation or whether it means 'in whatever way'. Indeed, the meaning of a sentence may change radically with the punctuation:

> The engines, which have been stripped down, are now in working order.
> The engines which have been stripped down are now in working order.

The first sentence, of course, refers to *all* the engines, while the second only to those which have been stripped down. Carried to extremes, confused punctuation can lead to very odd sentences, as in this real-life example:

> We have not included dampers unfortunately, not sufficient information available to enable accurate sizing however, as in the case of valves, we have provided motors and actuators.

Perhaps the writer intended:

> Unfortunately, we have not included dampers as we have insufficient information for accurate sizing. However, as in the case of valves, we have provided motors and actuators.

The reader, unfortunately, has to guess at the meaning. Punctuation is, however, less of a problem to the would-be writer than is spelling. Most punctuation obeys clear rules with rare exceptions, and it is worth learning at least the most helpful rules, which are probably to do with full stops and commas. The Bibliography (page 112) recommends books which will help and which have good examples; in this book we can point out only a few of the most common errors.

A sentence must, as we have said, make complete sense in itself, and it must contain a main verb:

> This being a delicate situation, if our clients decide to cut back on the project although at this stage our involvement is not great.

This is not a sentence, as there are three subordinate sections, that is, a part-verb 'being', a conditional clause 'if you decide', and a modifying clause 'although...is not great'. One of these must be made into a main verb if the words are to form a sensible sentence, and the most likely is that 'being' will become 'will be'. Again, if the original is read aloud, it can be heard not to make complete sense.

Probably more trouble is caused by the little word 'its' (or 'it's') than any other of comparable size in the English language. Apostrophes, it is often said, are an endangered species. Unfortunately their survival is often important to the meaning of a sentence. In the case of 'its'[b], the difficulty is easily overcome: if 'it is' or 'it has' is meant, then there is an apostrophe, and if it isn't, there isn't. (So: 'I've looked at the car and *it's* obvious that *its* tyres are reaching the legal limit.') There are only two uses of the apostrophe: to show where a letter is missed out (the 'i' in 'it is'), and to show possession. As the former use is inappropriate to a report ('it is' should always be written in full), only the possessive is likely to cause trouble. Usually, the sense will be clear whether the apostrophe is present or not, but sometimes the apostrophe is essential to the meaning:

> We have had many years of experience in dealing with our clients problems.

Many years with *one* client ('client's problems') or various clients ('clients' problems')? If we are interested in the experience, we will certainly want to know whether it is broadly-based or not. For this reason, the apostrophe is needed, and such cases should ensure that in formal writing at least, the apostrophe is kept alive.

40

The distinction between the colon and the semi-colon often bewilders the report writer. A colon is used to introduce a list of individual items, as in the following:

In order to conduct this experiment, we need the following equipment:
test tubes
retort
bunsen burners
reagents
litmus paper

It also introduces a quotation or example, as in the previous paragraph ('as in the following:'), or a list of points which have to be considered. So:

In reading the report, we noted the following observations:

1. that the contents list did not always agree with the contents provided;

2. that the standard of writing was not consistent with the gravity of the problem investigated;

3. that the binding broke after a few handlings, and pages fell out.

In this example, the precise rules for introducing the list have been followed: colon followed by continuations of the introductory sentence, each ending with a semi-colon, until the final point which concludes the sentence and ends with a full stop. However, in the list of items of equipment, given above, semi-colons would be cumbersome and have been omitted. If individual points are too long and in themselves contain complete sentences, then once more the system is broken:

The observations noted when the report was read are listed below.

1. The contents list did not always agree with the contents provided. A section on the use of diagrams is listed but could not be found, and the page references are wrong in at least three instances. Appendix C appears, strangely, before Appendix B.

Clearly, it would be peculiar to have a semi-colon after 'Appendix B', and the second point must start as a new sentence.

A semi-colon is almost as strong a pause as a full stop. It connects two complete sentences which are so strongly related in meaning (often contrast or paradox) that the writer wants to stress the link without joining them into one:

Old steam engines are to be seen, paint fresh and brass gleaming; the modern inter-city train may be faster, but it is dingy and uncared-for beside its forebear.

The contrast is more pointed because of the semi-colon. This is an elegant piece of punctuation and reads well, but too many semi-colons become heavy and lose their effect. Occasionally and judicially used, they are effective.

Grammar

This is not a grammar textbook (see Bibliography), and only a few common grammatical problems can be looked at. However, the writer of good reports will be constantly aware of the need for accurate grammar, and will notice, too, how helpful to the reader is a well-constructed, grammatically-correct report.

Problems can occur when a sentence changes construction mid-way:

Having conducted the experiment and being certain that my results were accurate and therefore I decided to write the article and see my efforts in print.

'Having conducted... I decided', or 'I had conducted the experiment... and therefore' would each be correct, but the two constructions should not be confused.

Unrelated participles are a common source of entertainment inappropriate to a report. In the previous example, 'Having conducted...' leads to the subject 'I', and it is clear that 'I' have conducted the experiment. 'Having' is a participle, not a complete verb, and it has to wait until after the comma for its subject to appear; that subject is usually the subject also of the main verb:

Having conducted the experiment... I decided to write...

(Participle)   (Subject) (main verb)

If the apparent subject of the participle is not the real subject, the result can be very odd:

Driving as fast as possible, the bridge came into view within an hour.

'Driving' is the participle and 'bridge' *appears* to be its subject and indeed *is* the subject of the main verb 'came', but it is unlikely that the bridge drove anywhere, quickly or otherwise. A particularly entertaining real-life example of the unrelated participle problem appeared in a guide book:

Having been thoroughly cleaned and renovated, visitors to the Cathedral will be impressed...

Poor visitors!

The confusion of singular and plural often results from a failure to identify correctly the subject of the sentence:

There is a wide range of materials available, which allow us to choose the most suitable for our purpose.

The subject of 'is available' is 'wide range', which is singular; the second part of the sentence must therefore begin 'which allows us...'. The problem word, of course, is 'materials', which is plural and which intervenes between subject and verb, and which is mistakenly thought of as the subject. 'Each' tends to create singular/plural confusion:

Each of the engineers concerned have written a report.

This is wrong, as the subject of 'have written' is 'each' (which means 'each one' and is therefore singular) and not 'engineers'. So:

Each of the engineers concerned has written a report.

Misuse of 'each' can again sometimes be entertaining:

There is a stretch of water between each bridge

presumably means that the river has flooded and each bridge is awash and highly dangerous! The sentence makes sense if 'and the next' is added, as water between two *bridges* is not uncommon.

Two common errors will complete this brief survey of grammatical problems. 'The reason is because' is unnecessary repetition, as clearly 'the reason' *is* 'because'. It is easily and wrongly written:

The reason that the project was a failure and had to be abandoned was because technical collaboration between the two countries concerned became impossible.

The writer has forgotten that he began with 'the reason', and so has felt the need to use 'because'. Correctly, the sentence could be either 'The reason that the project...was that technical collaboration...' or 'The project was a failure...because technical collaboration...', but not both at the same time.

A peculiarly treacherous word in spite of its size is 'only'. It must be placed as closely as possible to the word or words it refers to, as its position will affect the meaning of the sentence. If the sentence reads:

The financial manager offered me twice the salary I am currently receiving if I worked abroad for a year then we should certainly want to know, if we received such an offer, where 'only' might be placed. There are many possible positions, and if the sentence is read with each 'only' in turn, it is obvious that the offer becomes more or less attractive:

(Only) the financial manager offered (only) me (only) twice the salary (only) I am currently receiving if (only) I worked abroad for a year (only).

An example from a genuine report illustrates some of the problems of inaccurate writing:

The material certificates pages 5, 6 and 7 as your client has observed have dates 1983, 1984 and 1978 respectively, the latter is the vibrating spool for the density meter this is a very special alloy and can only be brought (*sic*) in bulk, and as such small quantities of material are used in each meter this certificate is relevant to the equipment supplied.

The problems are listed below.

1.	material certificates pages:	an apostrophe needed on 'certificates', but the phrase would read much more easily as 'pages 5, 6 and 7 of the material certificates'.
2.	as your client has observed:	easier to read if it is placed between commas. It is a comment on the rest, and we would read it aloud with a pause before and after.
3.	respectively:	this is the end of the first section of information, and should be followed by a full stop and a new sentence.
4.	the latter:	'the latter' describes the second of two items (the other being 'the former'). As there are three pages and dates mentioned, it is not clear whether 'the latter' refers to pages 6 and 7, or just page 7.

5. is the vibrating spool:	can a page (or indeed a date) be a vibrating spool? 'Is' presumably means 'refers to'.
6. density meter:	this is the end of the second section of information, and so should be followed by a full stop and a new sentence.
7. is (a very special alloy):	'is' would be clearer as 'is made of'.
8. very:	adds nothing to the meaning.
9. brought:	a typing error: read 'bought' (and see Chapter 6).
10. only:	a 'danger' word, as described above. Almost certainly, the writer meant that the alloy can be bought *only* in bulk, and not 'only bought'.
11. bulk:	this is the end of the third section of information, and so should be followed by a full stop and a new sentence.
12. as such:	there is nothing wrong with this expression, but we read it in two ways: 'as such small quantities', or 'as such,..'. If the ambiguity makes the reader go back and re-read the phrase, it would be better to write 'since'.
13. each meter:	should be followed by a comma for ease of reading.

The original passage may now be rewritten as follows:

Pages 5, 6 and 7 of the material certificates, as your client has observed, have dates 1983, 1984 and 1978 respectively. The last of these refers to the vibrating spool for the density meter, which is made of a special alloy obtainable only in bulk purchase. Since each meter takes only a very small quantity of material, this certificate remains relevant to the equipment supplied.

In rewriting this piece, we have assumed that the client had queried the early date (1978) of one of the certificates, and the report was intended to answer the query. No writing, however, should depend upon the reader's assumption of meaning, as the consequences of a mistaken assumption are too serious. Inaccurate or ambiguous expression costs money.

Paragraphs

If words can be gremlins and sentences locusts, there is no adequate term for the monstrous paragraphs which often appear in reports. It is depressing to turn over a page and to be faced with great chunks of print, with no opportunity for a pause or a feeling of satisfaction that one section at least has been read and understood. A paragraph usually deals with one aspect of the subject under discussion, and is as long as is necessary for that aspect to be covered adequately. At the same time, the average of three paragraphs to a page looks satisfactory and manageable to the reader. A compromise has to be reached. Reports tend to have shorter paragraphs than books or articles, and five or six paragraphs to a page is not unusual. The dictates of the subject matter and the ease of the reader are, as usual, the criteria on which decisions are based. For example, the following paragraph is difficult to assimilate because of the number of facts included (the facts are based on information provided by courtesy of the Motor Industry Information Service, which is operated by the Society of Motor Manufacturers and Traders):

More than 25 million people in Britain hold a driving licence. 8 out of every 10 tons of freight go by road. Each freight vehicle carries 3 times as much as its equivalent 30 years ago. 1% of passenger journeys are by bicycle. Britain has fewer motorways than France or Germany. More than half the British working population goes to work by car. The motor industry provides over a million jobs. 84% of passenger journeys are by private transport. Motor exports are second only to oil. More than 20 000 dealers and garages sell and service motor vehicles in Britain. Car ownership per thousand of population grew from 108 to 295 in Britain between 1960 and 1983.

The sentences are grammatically correct, although of a boringly uniform length, but the total effect of the paragraph is confusing. The material must be grouped according to aspect of the subject, each aspect providing a new paragraph. Aspects included are:

people and cars
motorways
freight carriage
exports
motor industry employment
bicycles

Some of these aspects, for instance people and cars/bicycles, are linked by contrast. Exports is too small an aspect to stand by itself, and it could provide a useful comment on the size of the motor industry (although a case could be made for putting it elsewhere). If the ideas are grouped in this way, the following passage might result:

> More than 25 million people in Britain hold a driving licence, and over half the working population goes to work by car. Indeed, 84% of passenger journeys are by private transport, of which only 1% is by bicycle. It is not surprising to learn that in Britain car ownership per thousand of population rose from 108 to 295 between 1960 and 1983.
>
> In spite of the fact that Britain has fewer motorways than either France or Germany, freight carriage is largely by road, eight out of every ten tons being transported in this way. Nevertheless, the efficiency of the system is shown by the fact that each freight transporter carries three times as much as its equivalent did 30 years ago.
>
> The motor industry is a major employer, providing over a million jobs. More than 20 000 dealers and garages sell and service motor vehicles in Britain. Motor exports are second only to oil.

These three paragraphs are short, clearly defined in material, and much more easily read and assimilated than the original. Careful paragraphing is important in producing reader goodwill.

Style

So far in this chapter, we have looked at some of the constituent parts of English usage: words, sentences, punctuation, grammar and paragraphs. If all these are used accurately, with the convenience of the reader in mind, the report will be acceptable and easy to use. It will not necessarily be a pleasure to read. Style is difficult to define, but it is essentially the manner of writing as opposed to the material. The first version of the motor transport facts given above was accurately written, but bad style; the revised version was accurate and much better in style, helpful to the reader and achieving a certain fluency. Good style comes largely from practice, not just practice at writing but also practice at criticism, at considering the good and bad points of reports, articles and books. The good ones should then be tried out, and the bad ones consciously avoided.

Reports are formal documents. They do not have to be pompous in style, or literary, but they do have to conform to a standard of business writing which is acceptable to the recipient. Within the formality, then, there are variations. A short note, sent to update the information a colleague already has, is comparatively informal. It must be grammatically correct to avoid ambiguity, but it may well use abbreviations ('we've had a look at the machinery, and in the light of what we found last time, you'll be pleased to know that...'). Such a message will probably be transmitted in the form of a memo. An in-company report which is intended for a number of people, including those higher in the hierarchy than the writer, is more formal. It does not use abbreviations, and should not contain slang, and it will be 'politically' acceptable, that is, it uses tact in the expression. 'We're getting fed up with the number of hold-ups in getting spares so we can't ever seem to get a move on' is the spoken word; 'We're always being held up for spares and it's causing frustration' might be the memo version; 'The lack of adequate spares provision is delaying output' would appear in the report. The slang 'fed up with' and the personal irritation have disappeared, while a clear objective statement of the problem has taken their place.

The level of formality is sometimes the subject of company policy. A report may be produced by 'me' or 'us' or 'the company', and the right usage is that demanded by the company's arbiters of taste. The choice is often between 'We recommend' and 'It is recommended that': the former is shorter and more direct, but the latter may be preferred because of its formality and its distancing of the individual from a company statement. Sometimes policy dictates that 'I' or 'we' is acceptable for internal reports but not for reports going outside the company. While this is obviously a decision for the individual organization, the report writer must be aware of the danger of changing a personal statement into an impersonal one: 'I cannot accept the idea' is different from 'The idea cannot be accepted', and it is usually true that the impersonal will be more wide-ranging than the personal: 'I suspect that...' is more limited than 'A suspicion may arise that...'

Writing in the active voice ('I recommend') is, as has been pointed out above, shorter and more direct than the passive ('It is recommended'). If there is a choice, the active is preferable for these reasons, as in this example:

We checked our figures and found the projected expenditure acceptable. (active: 10 words)
The figures were checked and the projected expenditure was found to be acceptable. (passive: 13 words)

Abstract words can be in themselves a barrier to understanding. The clearest, easiest writing is made up of precise, 'concrete' terms which the reader can visualize. In the following sentence, the abstract words: flexibility, keynote, policy, possibility, basis, intervals, variety and concentration, produce a dazed reaction in the reader, so that the simple message is lost:

Flexibility is the keynote to our company policy, and therefore where the possibility exists, workers are redirected on a rota basis at regular intervals to ensure variety and thereby to aid concentration.

If the abstract terms can be exchanged for precise, literal words, the sentence is immediately easier to understand:

This company believes that workers can concentrate more easily if they have a change of job every week or so. Where it is possible, therefore, a rota will be produced to give everyone variety in his or her work.

'Variety' is the only abstract idea remaining, and in the context of the two shorter sentences, its meaning is clear.

Good style is partly the result of logical thought. The old problem of the split infinitive ('to boldly go') shows an illogical approach to sentence structure.

After the alterations, it was possible to more easily move round the workshop.

The meaning is clear, but the infinitive ('to move') is one unit of the sentence, and the adverbial phrase ('more easily') refers to the whole idea of 'to move'. The sentence units should be brought together:

After the alterations, it was possible to move round the workshop more easily.

Nevertheless, English is a living language much less bound by rules and regulations than many other European languages, and one of its strengths is that if you know the rules, you are allowed to break them. Breaking the rules should be rare and carried out for an important reason, but with these provisos, the infinitive may be split:

It is essential to thoroughly disinfect the equipment.

Emphasis is thrown on the offending word 'thoroughly', which is presumably intended to carry great force, and in such a case, the breaking of the rule is justified. It follows, however, that such a sentence must be very unusual or the emphasis will be lost.

The mixed metaphor has no place in reports or any other writing, and it too follows from illogicality. Earlier in this chapter, we wrote of gremlin words and locust sentences: such writing would be inappropriate to a formal, objective report, but perhaps brightens a book *about* reports. If we had written:

A gathering of gremlin words produces a locust sentence

we should have been guilty of mixing metaphors: whatever the collective noun for gremlins is, it does not produce locusts! One despairing colleague was heard to say of another:

Every time he gets a bee in his bonnet he goes into it like a bull in a china shop

which mixes metaphors which are in themselves clichés, and so offends twice.

Such writing interrupts the reader, as do slang and jargon, because it draws attention to itself and away from the information to be conveyed. Abbreviations can have the same effect when they are inappropriately used. 'E.g.' and 'i.e.' are acceptable where a list of facts is given, or a number of examples or explanations, but in the middle of a piece of continuous prose the words should be written in full. 'For example' or 'that is' take very little longer to write, but allow the reader to move on without interference to the flow of the reading. Repetitive sentence or paragraph starts will also tend to distract the reader, and it is usually easy to avoid the problem by turning one sentence round. Two sentences in a paragraph or two paragraphs in a page may start with the same few words, but more than that will draw attention to an awkwardness of style.

On the other hand, linking words or phrases help the reader, not only improving the flow of the style but also guiding the reader in his approach to what follows. 'On the other hand', at the beginning of this paragraph, implied that what follows is a contrast to what has gone before (helping the flow rather than hindering it); 'in contrast' has a similar effect, while 'at the same time' suggests holding two points in tension, as does 'bearing in mind...'. Such words or phrases must be used carefully: 'Therefore' must introduce the logical consequence of what has just been written, while 'nevertheless' tells the reader to assume that in spite of what he has just read, there is another point to be considered. Linking words tell the reader how to order his mind for his approach to the next sentence or paragraph and although that ordering will usually be subconscious, it is important in encouraging him to read on.

The ability to write well is, as we said at the beginning of this chapter, a skill which results from an awareness of meaning and implication, and from hard work. Most writers, however experienced, feel a moment of panic when they are faced with a blank sheet of paper and the necessity of writing on it. 'Get started' is good advice, and in the case of report writing the start may be made at any point in the document. Often, the main body of the report with its factual evidence is a good place to begin: even if only one short section is available, write that section first. It may need revision later, but at least the psychological barrier is removed. The paper is no longer blank, and the report writer has proved that he can produce something. This is true for all writing, even if, as in the case of this chapter and indeed of this book, the first words are Shakespeare's.

CHAPTER 5

Data presentation

The fictitious James Bloggs, whose family's literary output was used as an example of reference-making in Chapter 3, works in Reading, but, for reasons outside the scope of this book, lives in West Drayton. Having had unpleasant experience of traffic congestion resulting, ironically, in a fine for speeding on one of the few mornings when the traffic was not congested, he decided to make the daily journey by train. Deadline at the office was half-past nine, and James set about finding how to get to work on time, through the services of British Rail. He elicited the following information.

The ideal train to catch in West Drayton in order to arrive in Reading by half-past nine is at seventeen minutes to nine. It is a through train to Reading, but it stops at Slough, Burnham, Taplow, Maidenhead and Twyford. It arrives at twenty-two minutes past nine, which allows James eight minutes to get clear of the station and to sprint across the road to the office. If he misses that train (and James is not the most alert of people early in the morning), then the next one departs at three minutes past nine and arrives in Reading at nearly a quarter to ten. Disastrous! It might be better to try to catch the twenty-three minutes past eight train which arrives at two minutes past nine. Another train from West Drayton leaves at twenty-seven minutes to nine, but goes only as far as Maidenhead. So if the train which leaves at twenty-three minutes past eight has gone, then the train which departs ten minutes later is no use and another ten minutes' wait is necessary before a train to Reading arrives at West Drayton.

Poor James! Faced with all this information, he would become totally confused. It is difficult to extract the times of departure and the times of arrival and easy to make mistakes in doing so (especially early in the morning). But of course James would not be faced with so much wordy material. He would go along to his local station and pick up a pocket timetable, in which all the details are set out in tabular form, and he would see at once which trains were available, and their time of arrival. Even at half-past eight in the morning, James would not be likely to make a mistake.

The same choice of presentation faces the report writer. A great deal of numerical information, or other complex detail, written in prose causes confusion, dismay and mistakes. Figures may be difficult to extract, and more time, which means also more money, will be needed for the reader to use the report material accurately. In this chapter, we will look at different ways of presenting information in a form which is easy to assimilate, that is, at diagrams, the word 'diagram' being taken to include tables, graphs and charts. With James' experience in mind, the report writer will want to save his readers' time by making the reception and assimilation of information as easy and as rapid as possible, and by reducing the possibility of error.

However, there is another side to diagrammatic presentation. If a diagram will not clarify the situation, then it should not be used. Only relevant and helpful diagrams have their place in a report. They are an integral part of the general presentation of the material, and should never be added as an afterthought, or to break up the prose and make the page look more interesting (which, incidentally, good diagrams do, as a by-product of their main function).

Convention and familiarity

If diagrammatic information is presented in an unusual or difficult format, it becomes a problem for the reader who, understandably, will ignore or reject it unless it is essential to his comprehension. If he finds it essential, he will struggle with and be irritated by it. On the principle of trying to gain reader goodwill, it is obviously important to avoid breaking the conventions with which the reader is familiar. Familiarity, it might be said, breeds assent, and the reader will readily accept and use a convention he has used before. For example, the form of a conventional clock face is so familiar that we can glance at it and read the time even if no figures appear on the dial: many clocks and watches have only marks to indicate the numbers. However, an anti-clockwise clock is a very different proposition. Many people, if shown a very clearly numbered clock face, on which the twelve numbers are written in an anti-clockwise circle, have difficulty in reading the correct time. Most can, and will, work out the rules for themselves and will obtain a reading. However, they will frequently mis-read the time by one hour, and rarely will they read it as quickly as they would from a conventional clock, when a mere glance is usually enough and mistakes are rare. The same problems occur with diagrams which break convention. They take longer to understand, and result in more mistakes. Clearly, it is in the writer's interest to produce a diagram which is easy to read and assimilate and which is comparatively error-free.

Sometimes, readers will convert information to a familiar format. People who recognise 75°F as indication of a fine day may not respond so cheerfully to 24°C. They may, if they know the formula, set about multiplying by 9 and dividing by 5 and adding 32 in order to get a familiar reading (and may make the mistake of adding 32 and then multiplying by 9 and dividing by 5). Similarly, 19.36 may be converted to 7.36 p.m. before it is understood. Information should, whenever possible, be presented in the format with which the reader is familiar and which he wishes to use. As usual with report writing, identifying the readership is important, and in the case of a varied readership it may well be appropriate to offer two versions of the same information, for example, metric measurements could be followed by their imperial equivalents in brackets.

When James Bloggs abandons the train from West Drayton to Reading, and goes on a walking holiday, he will be reassured by familiar landmarks which appear on his map: a roundabout, road junction or, of course, a pub. Reassurance is often sought by diagram users. One way of achieving such reassurance is to find an example where the value is known, and to follow it through. Once the path has been established, a similar one can be found for unknown data. With a mileage chart, for example, many people will check their usage by finding the distance between their home town and another town a known number of miles away. If their method proves to be correct, they will have the confidence to find the unknown distance for another journey. Although this kind of check should be unnecessary for a well-presented diagram, such reassurance is helpful, and where possible a familiar example should be included in a diagram.

Convention is important not only in presenting figures, but also in the use of signs, symbols and abbreviations. The most common and useful conventions are contained in British Standards and International Standards, and these should be followed whenever possible. Many company libraries have the British Standards relevant to employees, and libraries in further and higher education institutions also have sets of Standards (although not always complete sets), which are updated regularly by the staff. If the report writer is in doubt, it is always worth checking the Standard convention. Numbers in themselves must follow conventional use, and it is recommended that arabic numerals are always used, and roman numerals avoided, as the latter are too easy to confuse. Page numbers, numbered lists and so on should all use arabic numbers. British Standards also recognise both the full stop (.) and the comma (,) as representing a decimal point. Therefore, confusion may arise if the British habit of separating thousands from hundreds by a comma (for example, 11,236.95) is followed. Instead, it is recommended that a single space be left (for example, 11 236.95). If the number consists of four digits only, the space is considered unnecessary. However, some companies are concerned that when their figures represent sums of money, a space is dangerous as it could be filled by an extra digit, and so they retain the comma. The anxiety is a reasonable one, and so is acceptable provided, of course, that the convention used is made clear to the reader. Sometimes conventions develop of necessity, for instance, the confusion over the British use of the word 'billion' to mean a million million has now been clarified by British Standards and a billion, on both sides of the Atlantic, is one thousand million, 10^9.

Figures may be easier to read on the page when the type face has lining numbers, that is, when the tops and bottoms are level, as 1234, rather than non-lining numbers, such as 1234. Although the latter may sometimes look more attractive, they distract the eye from its horizontal line. The effect is particularly untidy when numerical information is presented in a table.

Dates, especially important in report writing (see Chapter 3), can be confusing if they are given in numerical form. Is 2.7.85 the second of July

1985 or the seventh of February 1985? Unless the convention used is made very clear, perhaps by columns headed D/M/Y, then the month must be written out in word form. In a formal report, it would be inappropriate to abbreviate the month to three letters, or to miss the first two numbers of the year: the acceptable form is 2 July 1985 (or, of course, 7 February 1985).

Report writers often need to use units of measurement, and again the British Standards should be followed. One abbreviation which gives particular trouble is m. In Britain, m has traditionally been used to represent miles (as in mph, miles per hour), and even the newest motorway signs give distances in miles abbreviated to m. The British Standard gives m as the abbreviation of metre, while a capital M is the Standard abbreviation for millions. There is no plural to such abbreviations, and s must not be added, for example 6 cm is correct, as cm represents both centimetre and centimetres. There should not be a full stop after such an abbreviation unless it occurs at the end of a sentence.

Occasionally, a report writer has a good reason (and there must be a good reason) for departing from British Standards (or, of course, from International Standards if the report is to be used elsewhere). It may be that the company's particular discipline uses terms not covered by the Standards, or that the company has abbreviations of its own which have a special significance within the industry. Where this happens, it is essential that the report user is told at the beginning of the report, in clearly set out prose which will attract his attention, that this is so. Indeed, where confusion might arise, it is worth stating that British Standards have been used throughout a report: at least the reader knows where to look if an abbreviation or a unit looks unfamiliar.

Data presented in a report must be in the most suitable format for the information and for the reader. Five common formats are used: tables, bar charts, pictograms, pie charts and graphs. Each will be considered in turn in the next part of this chapter, with its usage first, followed by the process and conventions used in producing the particular form.

Tables

Tables are probably the most common form of diagram in a report. They are used when there is a great deal of accurate information to be conveyed. Frequently this information is numerical, although it can also be verbal, for instance test results showing various properties of materials. The report writer must, as in every aspect of report production, consider the needs of the report reader or user, who may not want or be capable of handling all the detail available, and would much prefer numbers to be rounded off to the appropriate values. If he needs seven decimal places, then of course he must have them if at all possible, but if the writer has seven decimal places and the reader will be satisfied with one, then one is the correct number. More would only confuse the reader, and make the table more difficult to use. Of course it is tempting to give all the information available, especially if it has been particularly difficult to obtain, but if it is not required, it must not be included.

An over-complex table will be time-consuming for the user, and he might make mistakes in using it, although at the same time it must be remembered that the reader will also be irritated if he needs more detail than the table shows. The best advice is, as usual, to know the reader and to present the data appropriately.

When checking a list of equipment, we all find it much harder to scan along a row than down a column. For example, we might note down the basic requirements for a holiday under canvas as: canvas outer, inner compartments, groundsheet, pegs, mallet, guy ropes, poles, curtains and runners, trims, repair kits, storm pole, spares and clips. It is also useful to have chairs, table, cooker and stand, sleeping bags, airbeds, crockery, cutlery, pans, cleaning equipment and cold box.

As a list, the above is cumbersome and difficult to mark off. We should not find it a helpful checklist. However, as soon as the items are written in a vertical column, we have a list we can use easily and quickly:

Canvas outer
Inner compartments
Groundsheet
Pegs
Mallet
Guy ropes
Poles
Curtains and runners
Trims
Repair kit
Storm pole
Spares
Clips

and a secondary list of desirable items can then follow. Campers can also use this list as a check by counting the number of items, in this case an unlucky 13, which is difficult to do if they are listed across the page. Most writers creating a list will automatically choose a vertical format.

This convention is important when the report writer is creating a table of information. Details which are to be scanned should be presented vertically, while related items should be presented horizontally. The direction of scan is from top to bottom and the direction for reading horizontally (at least in the Western world) is from left to right. For example, a scientist interested in the properties of a particular material would need to scan down a list of materials until he found the one he required and then horizontally along the row to read the properties. Tables which do not adhere to this format are confusing and difficult to use.

Space is the ally of diagram-makers, and especially of those who produce tables. Report readers do not enjoy being made to walk across pages with their fingers in order to make both column and row meet: it looks childish and it can easily lead to a mistake. Space is the answer. If the vertical list is broken by space after every five, or at most seven, items, then it is not difficult to identify the particular item needed. Turk and Kirkman[4] have suggested that this happens because we can identify up to five objects placed in a group without counting them. Some people can manage six or seven, but it is more usual to break such groups down into two groups of three or groups of four and three. The smaller the chance of the reader's eye slipping from a line in a table, the smaller is the chance of incorrect information being extracted.

Vertical space helps in the same way. Often, tables begin their lives as grids drawn on a page, into which the figures are fitted. This may initially help their creator, but it is rarely helpful for the user to find the grid on the finished product. A vertical line breaks the information on the horizontal line, and unless this is necessary for the material to be understood, it should be avoided. Generally, vertical space is more helpful than a ruled vertical line. Horizontal lines may be ruled under headings to separate them from the data, and could be ruled above and below totals on the bottom line, or above and below the table to separate it from the text, but horizontal lines between items in the vertical list are unnecessary, and distract the reader's eyes from the information.

Each column of a table should have a clear, succinct heading, which precisely indicates the information below. Whenever possible, column headings should be presented horizontally, as they are then easy to read. However, if it is necessary to slope the headings, because of the amount of information in a table, then they should be sloped in such a way that turning the page through 90° or less, in a clockwise direction, will bring them into horizontal alignment. While this can be a useful device, it may present problems for the typist unless he has specialist equipment. Headings should not in any case be centred on a column, but aligned with the left hand edge of the column while numbers should be aligned under the decimal point, that is, hundreds under hundreds and tens under tens. Column headings should include, where appropriate, the units of measurements and powers of ten, for instance, to express millions, thousands and thousandths. Such abbreviations are common in the headings of financial tables.

Thousands

Home Population

	United Kingdom¹			England and Wales		Wales		Scotland¹		Northern Ireland	
	Persons	Males	Females	Males	Females	Males	Females	Males	Females	Males	Females
All ages	56 376.8	27 430.2	28 946.6	24 244.2	25 519.4	1 361.0	1 446.2	2 485.0	2 665.4	772.5	806.0
0 – 14	11 170.2	5 733.9	5 436.4	4 917.2	4 659.5	281.9	266.4	535.5	508.7	205.3	195.4
15 – 64	36 789.6	18 396.3	18 393.3	16 390.3	16 322.7	907.2	911.7	1 672.5	1 704.7	492.9	496.4
65 and over	8 417.0	3 299.9	5 116.8	2 936.7	4 537.2	171.9	268.1	277.0	452.0	74.3	114.2
0 – 4	3 582.0	1 836.8	1 745.2	1 605.6	1 527.0	91.3	86.6	168.4	159.6	68.8	66.0
5 – 9	3 364.3	1 728.2	1 636.1	1 498.4	1 417.3	86.0	80.8	161.3	153.1	64.7	61.8
10 – 14	4 223.9	2 168.9	2 055.1	1 813.2	1 715.2	104.6	99.0	205.8	196.0	71.8	67.6
15 – 19	4 729.1	2 430.4	2 298.6	2 077.1	1 973.2	116.5	112.6	231.2	220.8	76.3	70.6
20 – 24	4 499.3	2 275.7	2 223.6	2 059.6	2 005.2	114.2	113.7	220.1	211.0	71.3	65.5
25 – 29	3 893.0	1 962.8	1 930.2	1 763.8	1 727.9	91.2	88.8	186.6	182.3	56.1	56.3
30 – 34	3 847.5	1 934.7	1 912.8	1 690.8	1 667.0	91.0	89.9	173.3	171.2	49.9	49.1
35 – 39	4 023.4	2 018.7	2 004.7	1 829.5	1 817.2	98.2	98.6	171.6	171.0	49.2	49.6
40 – 44	3 246.7	1 632.5	1 614.4	1 487.5	1 461.8	83.5	81.8	145.1	149.5	44.0	44.8
45 – 49	3 118.2	1 564.0	1 554.2	1 400.5	1 384.6	77.8	76.8	141.2	147.8	39.1	40.8
50 – 54	3 115.3	1 544.3	1 570.9	1 350.8	1 358.2	76.0	77.0	139.7	150.5	36.7	39.7
55 – 59	3 142.2	1 535.4	1 606.8	1 347.4	1 396.8	78.2	81.6	136.5	149.8	35.7	39.7
60 – 64	3 174.9	1 497.8	1 677.1	1 383.3	1 530.8	80.6	90.9	127.2	150.8	34.6	40.3
65 – 69	2 567.7	1 154.9	1 412.7	979.6	1 185.8	59.8	73.3	98.5	128.5	26.9	34.1
70 – 74	2 402.1	1 012.7	1 389.4	907.8	1 233.3	52.8	72.7	86.1	124.3	23.1	32.4
75 – 79	1 771.6	662.3	1 109.2	607.8	1 003.2	34.4	59.0	55.2	97.9	14.3	23.8
80 – 84	1 039.6	322.6	717.0	304.4	660.9	17.0	38.2	25.9	61.7	6.7	14.5
85 and over	636.0	147.4	488.5	137.1	454.0	7.9	24.9	11.3	39.5	3.3	9.4

Note: Figures may not add due to rounding.

¹ 1983 figures.

Figure 5.1 *Tabulated data*

Sources: Office of Population Censuses and Surveys, General Register Office (Scotland), General Register Office (Northern Ireland) (Reproduced with the permission, of the Controller of Her Majesty's Stationery Office)

Figure 5.1, Tabulated Data, is an illustration of a well-presented table not from a report but from a book of statistical tables in which, unusually, numbers and titles are more appropriately placed above than below the diagrams. Although it is of necessity given in printed form, its good qualities could be applied equally to typed work. These desirable qualities are listed below.

1. To make each number more compact, it has been divided by one thousand and rounded to one decimal place.

2. Column headings are aligned to the left-hand edge of the column.

3. Horizontal lines have been ruled only to separate headings and totals.

4. Rows have been grouped, with space left between every three or five items, or to identify a single item when appropriate.

5. Lining numbers have been used.

6. There are no ruled vertical lines.

7. The numbers are aligned under the decimal points.

8. Space has been left between the thousands and the hundreds.

Bar charts

Bar charts are frequently used to show trends and variations. This is their primary purpose, and they should therefore not be made too complex: the information must be available at a glance. No more than two items should be compared on a single bar chart; if three items are needed, then three bar charts, with identical scales, drawn on the same page, will give this information more clearly than one bar chart which tries to cover all three. Bar charts drawn for comparative purposes must always have the same scale, or they will give the user a false impression of the comparison.

Although bar charts cannot give precise information, they must still be drawn as accurately as possible, each bar being carefully measured. Including the accurate figures alongside the bars is helpful and recommended, but even then the user will retain the visual impression rather than the numerical values, and the two must not conflict. Information which is continuous should be represented by adjoining bars, for example, a chart showing annual rainfall, subdivided into monthly amounts, should be drawn with connecting bars. Obviously, August's rainfall starts where July's rainfall stops. On the other hand, discrete information should be shown by bars separated by space, for example, population figures counted once every five years should be shown by bars separated to show the missing years. Obviously, the population will not remain constant from the beginning of 1980 to the end of 1984.

Bars may be drawn either vertically or horizontally, preferably in such a way that the diagram has an overall landscape shape (see p. 66). Shading is sometimes used to distinguish the bars, but this is a practice which requires great care if unexpected results are not to appear (see Optical illusions, p. 67).

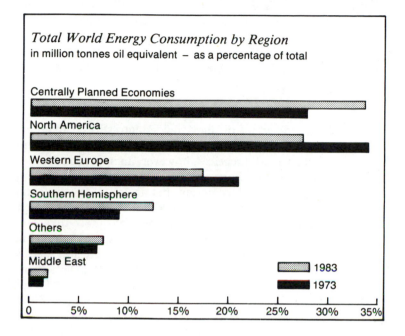

Figure 5.2   *Bar chart*

Source: *Barclays Review*, May 1985. (Reproduced with kind permission of British Petroleum Company p.l.c.)

The example shown in Figure 5.2 has been chosen as an illustration of how a bar chart can be used effectively. Its good qualities are listed below.
1.   It shows only two items, 1973 and 1983.
2.   The accurate figures are shown on the scale.
3.   The bars give discrete information, and therefore each pair is separated from the others.
4.   The diagram is clearly labelled.
5.   The overall shape of the bar chart is landscape.

Pictograms

Tables and bar charts are successful for a readership which understands their use and is capable of handling the information given. However, many people dislike figures, and will be nervous of or will even avoid reading numerical data. If it is appropriate, the report writer can help such readers by using pictograms to show the necessary information in the form of pictures rather than numbers. This can be very effective, especially when details have to be presented to the general public, or in advertising literature. However, pictograms look childish and patronizing in a formal business report, and should never be used in such a context.

A further difficulty of pictograms is their production. Hand-drawn pictograms are unlikely to look professional, which means that the author must be or must employ a good artist, or must have a graphics department available to him. Even so, the finished impression can distort the information presented, and care is needed to make sure that the reader gets the right message.

Pie charts

Pie charts are circular diagrams or 'pies' divided into slices, each representing a sub-division of the original amount. They emphasise divisions and proportions to the reader, who receives, however, an impression rather than a detailed picture. As with bar charts, so pie charts must be drawn accurately, with precise values written on the diagram, but again it is the visual impression which lasts. For this reason, a pie should not be too complicated, and it is better to have two pie charts than one which has more divisions than the eye can cope with. Five slices is usually a sensible maximum. The difference in size between slices must be obvious to the user, and slices which are too close in size will be seen as identical: differences of less than 7° at the centre of segments will not be apparent to the report reader. The picture is often clearer if the sizes are arranged clockwise, starting at 12 o'clock, in descending order of size. It is also helpful if small slices are placed horizontally, so that their labels can be written in a horizontal line, but clearly these two criteria may conflict, and the report writer must decide which is paramount in any particular case. A different form of diagram closely related to the pie chart is the percentage bar chart, in which a bar representing 100 per cent is used in place of a circle. It is divided into sections rather than slices, and although it is easier to draw than a pie chart, it makes less impact.

Graphs

If tables are the most common form of diagram in a report, graphs are probably in second place. They have two distinct uses: they can give accurate scientific or similar results, and they can be used to show trends. If the data given are precise, it can be useful to give a table showing the points plotted on the graph, indeed, it may be important to do so. In principle, two versions of the same diagram are not recommended, and certainly it does not follow that if one version is unclear, the other will remove the confusion. Nevertheless, the presentation of scientific detail in both graphical and tabular forms can be an important exception to the general principle, and an aid to understanding.

Graphs are, not surprisingly, usually drawn on graph paper. This comes in different colours and types, but normally shows millimetre squares which are rarely needed by the user. Indeed, these millimetre squares can be a positive disincentive to using the graph, as they tend to produce a murky background, especially if the graph is photocopied. There is an easy way out of this difficulty. The report writer uses a sheet of graph paper the grid of which will not photocopy (pale grey is usually good for this purpose) and, after drawing his graph, he provides the user with the photocopy without the grid and retains the original with the grid for himself. If some of the grid lines will be helpful to the reader, then they can be inked in: the producer of the report must again assess what the reader will need.

When the axes of the graph have been drawn and the scales carefully selected and marked, the known points may be plotted. If intermediate values, which have not been measured, can be relied upon to be good estimates, then the plotted points should be connected by a smooth curve. Take, for example, an average sunflower. Each week its height is measured and recorded on a graph. Sunflowers tend to conform to a regular pattern of growth, and it is likely that an average sunflower will therefore follow an upward trend: it is unlikely that between measurements the plant has either shot up and then shrunk or shrunk and then shot up again. Intermediate measurements on the graph are likely, give or take a millimetre or two, to be valid, and the points on the graph will be joined by a smooth curve.

However, all graphs do not follow the sunflower norm. If intermediate values may not be relied upon, then adjacent plotted points should be connected by ruled straight lines, forming what is known as a straight-line graph. Take, for example, unemployment figures recorded annually. Such figures vary from season to season, and a measurement taken at the same time of each year will mask up and down variations in between recordings. The graph must therefore be straight-line, the line itself being drawn only to assist the eye. The convention of smooth curves and straight lines in graphs is widely understood and accepted and it should always be followed.

The example given in Figure 5.3 (see page 62) has been chosen as an illustration of how a graph can be effectively presented. Its good qualities are listed below.

1. The scientific results shown on this graph will be discussed fully in the text, and are not therefore duplicated on the diagram itself. Essential notes have been kept to a minimum: it is, however, reasonable to explain A and B.

2. The lines A and B are labelled at the end of each curve.

3. Apart from the essential plotted points and lines, and the letters A and B, no material is added within the diagram. The illustrator has resisted the obvious temptation to write notes in the space at the lower right-hand corner of the graph.

4. The lines are distinguished by thickness and not by colour.

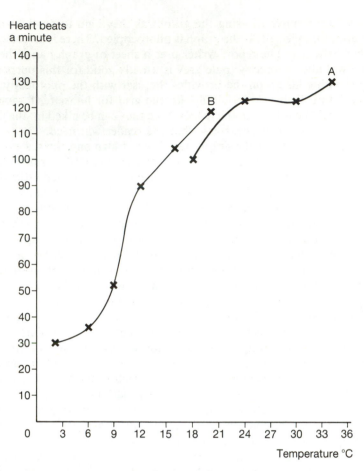

Heart beats a minute

A: Increasing temperature

B: Decreasing temperature

Figure 7.2   Effect of increasing and decreasing temperatures on the rate of heartbeat in tadpoles

Figure 5.3   *Graph*

5. The background grid has been omitted (although some of it could be drawn in if it were required).

6. The scales are clearly marked in a horizontal position. There is no risk of 'upside-down' writing if the graph were to be bound into the report in the landscape position (see page 66).

7. The figure number and title are printed below the diagram, in such a position that confusion with the vertical scale is impossible.

8. A good margin on all sides of the figure enhances its appearance and prevents 'disappearance' into the binding.

While graphs are a useful and informative way of presenting data, they can be used, deliberately or otherwise, to mislead. A scale can be chosen which distorts the results (for instance, a vertical scale which does not begin at zero) so that the graph represents only a small part of the overall picture, and the trend shown is exaggerated. Occasionally, the vertical scale is omitted altogether, so that the graph line can be as steep or as level as its creator chooses. Two graphs which present similar information but which use different scales will appear to be a comparison of data, but will in fact mislead. In a report, it is essential that the user receives accurate information, and all such 'tricks' should be avoided.

The five most widely used forms of diagram have been discussed in this chapter, but even when the most appropriate forms have been chosen, and clearly and accurately produced, the problem of data presentation is not finished. There are still decisions to be made about the positioning of diagrams, their headings and notation, and checks to be made of their clarity to the user: they are usually clear enough to the person who has drawn them.

Positioning of diagrams

Diagrams should appear in a report where they are needed, that is, the convenience of the reader should again be paramount. If, as the reader works on the report, he will understand the situation more readily by looking at the diagram, then the diagram should be in the text at the point at which he will want to look at it. If he is asked to 'turn to page 21', or even to turn overleaf, he will probably continue to read the prose unless or until it becomes essential for him to look at the diagram, by which time he may already be confused by what he has read, and he will be irritated at having to search for the diagram. Sometimes the opposite problem occurs, and a diagram gets in the way of the reader because it breaks up the text. Long tables showing experimental or other results, for example, may be better placed at the end of the report in an appendix than in the text, where the reader would forget the prose as his attention is deflected by rows of figures. Prose should never be broken abruptly, especially in mid-sentence, by a diagram.

Ideally, the diagram should be introduced, presented and discussed. If the diagram is referred to several times in the same report, then the writer has to decide whether to place it at the end, for overall convenience, or possibly to add it to a fold-out sheet which can be seen from any stage of the document. Diagrams which are not essential to the main readership of the report, but which are helpful to a minority, should appear in an appendix. Wherever diagrams are finally placed, the text must make their position absolutely clear, and no diagram or illustration should appear anywhere in a report if it is not referred to in the text.

Titles and numbers

Any diagram which does appear in the text must be clearly titled and numbered. As with report titles and headings (see Chapter 3), diagram titles should be as brief as possible, clearly stating what the diagram is about, without giving a full description. Titles should also clearly be titles, not placed in such a position that they appear to be labels on the illustration. The worst offence is to use up a space which occurs at the side of the diagram, when it can be unclear which diagram the title belongs to. The best position is underneath the diagram, and the most important rule is to be consistent in the positioning of titles throughout a report or series of reports.

Diagrams must have numbers as well as titles, for easy positioning and identification. The simplest, and therefore the best, method is to call all diagrams, whatever their form, Figures, and to give them two numbers separated by a decimal point. The first number will be the number of the major section in which the illustration occurs (as all diagrams in this chapter are identified by the first number, 5), and the second is the sequential number. So, Figure 5.7 is the seventh illustration in the fifth section of the report. It does not matter that Figure 5.7 appears in sub-section 5.2, or even sub-section 5.3.6: only the major section number is used. If the diagram appears in an appendix, then the identifying letter of that appendix precedes the numbers. So, Figure B3.2 is the second illustration in section 3 of Appendix B. The figure number should always precede the title of the figure, and be on the same line.

House styles about diagram labelling and positioning may have to take precedence over many of the recommendations made above. The practice of placing all diagrammatic material at the end of the report, irrespective of the reader's convenience, may initially save money, but it is to be deplored and, whenever possible, resisted. Sometimes the house style requires tables to be numbered separately from other figures (or even graphs and tables to be separate from each other and from the rest of the diagrams), but this can lead to confusion, for example between Table 3.2 and Figure 3.2, and it is not recommended. Whatever makes the diagrams easy to locate and easy to use is always worthwhile in terms of reader goodwill.

Diagram production

The text of a report is usually clear and easy to read. It is typed or word processed, and individual letters are distinct and present the reader with few problems. However, although few people would present a handwritten report, a surprising number present reports with handwritten labels on the diagrams, causing unnecessary trouble to the reader. The diagram should first be drawn, using a drafting pen filled with black ink, and an appropriately sized nib, such as 0.5 mm or 0.7 mm. The advantage of a drafting pen is that it will draw all lines at a constant thickness, while other types of pen produce variations in thickness which look untidy, particularly after reproduction. A4 size drawing boards should be used to ensure that lines really are parallel or at right angles. When the drawing is completed, but still without labels or numbers, it should be photocopied. Onto this copy, all labels, scales, numbers and any other items can be handwritten, and both photocopy and original given to the typist, who can then see the information to be produced, and where the labels should appear. He can then type these onto the original.

If shortage of space means that some labels must be sloped, they should be angled in such a way that turning the page through a maximum of 90° in a clockwise direction will bring them into horizontal alignment. As this will probably cause problems for the typist, the labels may have to be produced with the aid of a product such as Letraset, or by using a drafting pen and matching stencil. In the case of graphs needed without their original grid, the original should be marked by hand and the typist should then type onto the copy.

Photocopying

Copies of reports are usually produced by photocopying. If the original is clearly typed, then all the copies will be clear and easy to read. However, if there is a slight loss of clarity in the photocopying, and a letter becomes blurred or faint, the reader has to rely on the context in order to recognize the missing letter. Normally this causes little difficulty, and the reader will often read the word without even realizing that one letter is not clear. (This is not, of course, recommended, and the enormous problem of checking will be discussed in more detail in Chapter 6.) The more serious problem arises when a number is unclear. The context will probably offer no clue as to what it should be, and if it is misread, the results might be very serious indeed, in either technical or financial terms. Some figures are particularly prone to confusion: 6, 8 and 5 quickly become indistinguishable, for example. If a number is sufficiently important to be included in a report, it must be read accurately. The report writer is not the best judge of the clarity of either words or numbers: as he wrote them in the first place, he knows what they should be, and will tend to read what he knows, rather than what he sees. He would be wise to ask a colleague to read the numbers aloud while he follows them on the page.

Since most photocopying is still black and white, it is best to produce the original report in black and white. If colours are photocopied, the result can be a murky grey. However, if the report is printed, then it may be possible to use colour for some diagrams, although the cost of production will be much higher. There are other problems apart from the financial. Many men are colour blind to some extent, and the most commonly 'lost' colours are red and green: these particular colours should be avoided, especially if two items have to be differentiated by colour. Printed colours are not always the same as their originals, and again clear differentiation may be lost in the printing. It is always worth discussing the choice of colour with the printer. Another consideration to be borne in mind is that report users are often not working with the report in natural light: fluorescent light or the greenish light of some visual display units can 'change' the colour on the printed page.

Space and shape

A page of typed or printed prose is usually neatly presented, with space at the top and bottom of the page and sensible margins to left and right. The writing is framed by space (although in passing, it is worth noting that the right hand justification of type is less favoured than it used to be, with the general feeling that a 'ragged' edge is easier to read). This spacing of the page looks pleasant, it also allows room for the page number and a running title if there is one, and it prevents words being lost in the binding of the report. For some reason, this frame is often ignored if the page contains only diagrammatic material. The frame is just as important, as the page number must still be clear, and the diagram number and title should appear as a distinct entity with space underneath them. When numbers on diagrams collide with page numbers, confusion and, what is worse, errors can occur. In the same way, diagrams which disappear into the binding look untidy, and potentially important material is hidden. Lines on a graph should end at their frame, and not overflow onto the desk.

Space is also helpful within the diagram, assisting the eye to take in the information presented. The report writer should never be tempted to fill an empty area of a graph with words, or to add too much detail so that the reader is confused. The advantage of vertical and horizontal space in tables has already been discussed (see p. 56). However, misuse of space is also confusing. If too much space is left between related items, the eye may lose track across the page, as happens sometimes on the contents page of a book, where the chapter headings are at the extreme left hand edge and the page numbers are far to the right. Indeed, if a larger space is left between related items than between unrelated items, the reader will search for the non-existent connection between the unrelated items.

We accept readily what is pleasing to the eye, often without realizing why we are doing so. It has been discovered that when a picture is presented in a landscape format (that is, with the horizontal edge longer than the vertical edge), it is more acceptable to the viewer than when it is presented in a portrait format (that is, with the horizontal edge shorter than the vertical edge). Therefore, the overall shape of a diagram should whenever possible be landscape. Often this can be achieved without turning the document, that is, when the diagram occupies less than a full page. If the document has to be turned, the turn must be in a clockwise direction, so that on a right hand page a turned diagram will have its top towards the binding, while on a left hand page the bottom will be towards the binding.

An unfortunate result of mishandling the diagram position is the phenomenon known as 'upside-down writing'. This is surprisingly common. Usually, the vertical scale on a graph or table has been written at 90° to the diagram, and the finished product has then been turned 90° and put into the report. The words have now travelled a full 180° and thus appear upside-down. The immediate impact of this is entertaining, but the humour is, like the writing, misplaced.

All information in a report should be clear to the intended reader.

Diagrams are usually clear to their creator, who has after all spent considerable time and effort in producing them. They may be totally obscure or, perhaps more dangerously, ambiguous to the reader. The best way to check that the diagrams are clear is to beg or bribe a colleague to extract the information. If he can, then the reader probably can, too.

Optical illusions

'The best laid plans...' Even when the diagram creator has taken time and effort to select the right format and to produce a clear, well-organized diagram, the result may not have the desired effect because the eye of the user has been deceived by an optical illusion.

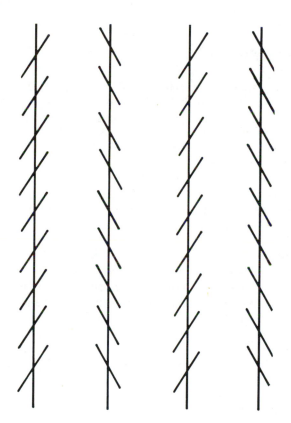

Figure 5.4 *'Non-parallel' lines*

A well-known example of this problem is shown in Figure 5.4. Adjacent parallel lines are cross-hatched in opposite directions, and the effect produced is of lines which are not parallel. The same illusion can occur when bar charts have alternated hatching. Even though the bars are in fact parallel, the effect is untidy.

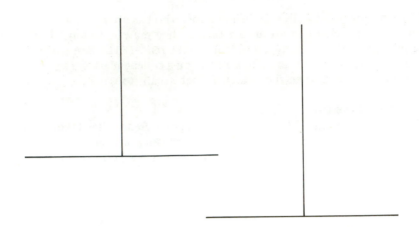

Figure 5.5 *Equal lengths*

Another, less well-known, effect is shown in Figure 5.5. It is not obvious to the viewer which vertical line is the same length as the base line. One consequence of this illusion is that if a title is to be centred vertically on a page, actually measuring the centre will give the effect of a dropped title. It will appear to be below the centre in spite of the measurement. Centring, therefore, has to be above the measured centre line.

Another strange effect is caused by closely ruled parallel lines. These tend to show movement where clearly no movement is possible. Owners of striped blouses or shirts (or their friends and colleagues) will be aware of the dazzling effect they cause!

Conclusion

The principles outlined in this chapter for achieving clarity in diagrams apply to other illustrations as well as those discussed. If a diagram is worth including in a report, even in the appendix, then it must be clear and usable. Blurred copies of photographs, regulations or computer print-outs are sometimes included in reports, or pages of advertising literature are poorly copied and added as appendices. If the material will not copy successfully, it must be produced in some other way, or omitted. Regulations, or complete print-outs with very small print or produced on a dot matrix printer, should be re-typed. Photographs must be clear, and black and white: if they cannot be copied successfully, they should be left out.

Some companies have arrangements for printing illustrations, and advice will be given about the preparation of copy. Even if such facilities exist, they are very expensive, and the writer of a small, in-company report might have to resort to do-it-yourself. For all producers of diagrammatic material, there is one final warning. You are responsible for abiding by the laws of copyright, and any illustration taken from a published document may be reproduced only with permission from the copyright holder.

CHAPTER 6

Revision and checking

In the middle of writing words and preparing diagrams, the producer of reports might think that he was fully occupied, and that revision was something that happened later, if there was time. He would be sadly mistaken. Revision of a report starts when the format (Chapter 3) is chosen and the material is organized, stages which, as we have seen, precede the writing. The writing itself may not begin at the beginning, which is another good reason for constant revision until the last available moment.

Meeting the objectives

The report writer will have identified his readership and clarified his terms of reference. He will probably have written out the objective of the report in a sentence or a short paragraph. People being people, he may well forget all of this as he is carried away by the most original, impressive, interesting or simply time-consuming aspects of the work. Revision is, then, the checking back, the regular reference to all those initial decisions in order to make sure that the report is still going in the right direction. It is easy to be side tracked. A group of students, asked to write a report 'selling' their home town as a site for relocation to a 'company' which was considering Edinburgh as an alternative, found that they knew a good deal about the facilities offered by the town they worked in, but that they had to put time and effort into finding out about the counter-attractions of Edinburgh. Unfortunately, they were so carried away by their own initiative and information-seeking that they ended up by producing reports which 'sold' Edinburgh. It was as well for their future employment that the reports were part of an exercise and not part of 'real life'!

The danger is a real one, however. Reports which cover a limited geographical area may wander outside their limits; reports may stress the problems at the expense of the recommendations; they may recommend what is technically appropriate while overlooking the personnel implications. The balance of the report has to be revised to make sure that it is the balance originally intended, and that the writer's enthusiasm (or indeed distaste) has not prejudiced the outcome.

Clarification of headings

It is also necessary to revise the headings. As was suggested in Chapter 3, the original general headings usually have to be made more specific, to ensure that they are as helpful as possible to the report user. They may also need to be re-arranged, to make their logical progression helpful and clear; the information within a section may need to be moved around to produce a more efficient result, and even the words in a sentence may be changed in order to produce the correct emphasis.

Checklist for revision

If the report production takes a week, the writer may sensibly spend half an hour each day revising what has been prepared and asking if there is any better way to present the information than the way he has chosen. A good way of answering the question might be to take a 'purple passage', the section of which the writer is most proud, and to subject it to the following analysis:

Is this relevant to what I am trying to do?

Is this relevant to what the reader/user will want?

Does this passage fit into the pattern of the whole report?

Is the organization clear, logical and easy to use?

Is the material divided into manageable chunks (sections, sub-sections or paragraphs)?

Does each sentence add to the meaning—and is it grammatically correct?

Does each word add to the meaning—and is it used precisely?

Will the reader/user *also* consider this to be a highlight of the report?

If the honest answer to any of these questions is 'no', then revision is clearly called for. It will in the long run save time (that of the authorizing authority, the typist, the client) and will bring about a faster response.

In-company considerations

Revision by the report writer is a good thing; revision by the writer's superior may be questioned. It is often helpful, especially if the supervisor (branch head, head of department or whoever) discusses with the writer the changes which are required, or at least adds positive comments to the work which has been produced. It is not at all helpful if changes are made to the writer's style, not because it is bad, but because it is different from that of the superior. Writing style is an individual matter and, while house style should be adhered to, changes to an acceptable personal style can be hurtful. They may also be counter-productive, as they are often obvious to the reader, who may be disturbed in his reading by a sudden and inexplicable change of reading pattern. While it is often useful to have technical and legal content checked by a higher authority, and any ambiguity or illogicality questioned, change for the sake of change (the 'I must make my mark' syndrome) is bad for morale. The young engineer who comments sadly that his report no longer says what he meant it to say *and he doesn't know why*, may well resent his superior's attitude and lose confidence in his own work. Of course 'political' considerations will weigh heavily on more senior staff, but a few words of explanation (or indeed an explanation that an explanation is impossible for reasons of confidentiality) will help junior staff to accept what at first sight seems to be meaningless interference.

Confidentiality

Confidentiality is an important consideration in the production of reports, for various reasons. The information contained in the report may be highly sensitive, possibly affecting national security. It may include research data which are confidential to the company whose scientists produced the report, or financial details which could be useful to a rival company. Reports often have commercial implications, and are at least temporarily confidential to a small number of people. In such cases, it is essential to record the number of existing copies of a particular report, with each copy stating clearly which number it is, and of what total. Library records may not show that the report exists (although clearly some record must be kept of the whereabouts of all copies), or may indicate the existence of the report but show also that it is not available for general use. However, confidentiality extends beyond the company responsible for the report: it may include information provided by outside bodies which do not wish to be identified. The normal acknowledgement of outside help must then be omitted, but the revision of the report should include a careful check that confidentiality has not been breached by accident. Reference to a particular product might identify a research establishment; a photograph of a notable building will identify architect, construction company and possibly a wide range of sub-contractors, to other people in the same industry. If the report writer has the slightest hesitation about including confidential material, he has a moral obligation to check with the source, just as the 'real-life' examples used in this book are given only with permission from the original companies. There is, naturally, an obligation to treat the resulting information as a confidential document while the report writing is in progress: it is not unknown for report writers and readers to feel 'safe' on a commuter train, regardless of the unusually close proximity of unknown fellow-travellers!

Checking the text

In an ideal world, each important report would be checked by two people, neither of them the author. The first would check the accuracy of the information and the suitability of its presentation: he would know a good deal about the material of the report, although preferably slightly less than the author. The second would know nothing at all about the information given, but would check the typed report against the manuscript (or the first typed draft), to catch typing errors. Both would have plenty of time in which to carry out these duties, which would be recognized as important stages in the production of a report.

Even in a world far from ideal, it is still worthwhile to have the most prestigious (or expensive) reports checked in this way. Inaccurate information will undermine confidence in a company's technical expertise. Perhaps surprisingly, so will typing errors. The reader may reasonably feel that an organization of high reputation and advanced technology will know its facts, and that the error which produces 'modern' for 'modem' will be recognized for what it is, a slip of the typewriter (or word processor, or someone's illegible handwriting). However, the reader may feel less reasonable on finding details of costing given with the heading, 'The prices listde below...'. Both these examples are real-life, as is that of the typist who transformed 'There is *not* a substantial amount of water in the brickwork' into 'There is *now* a substantial amount of water in the brickwork.' No computer spell-check (a widespread 'get-out clause') would pick up such a mistake, but its effects could be highly damaging to a company's professional reputation.

The technical content is usually checked, by superiors or well-disposed colleagues; the frequently forgotten aspect is the typing. Word processors tend, against popular opinion, to increase the problem of typing errors. Just because it is easy to change a word or a sentence, without the need to re-type the page, word processor operators sometimes check less thoroughly. So too do report writers, on whom the final responsibility rests. Some of the problem results from the failure, widespread in the UK although not necessarily in other countries, to involve the secretary in the production of a report. If the secretary understands the logic of decimal notation, realizes the importance of checking the whole report (diagrams as well as words) and can assess the impact of the document in its entirety (good, clear title page, sufficient margin space, and so on), then he can contribute effectively to the presentation of the report, not least by pointing out mistakes when they occur. Too often, pages are handed over without explanation for a secretary/typist to copy: the better the secretary, the more likely he is to become bored or frustrated, and the greater the number of mistakes which will not only be made, but which will live on, unchecked. A secretary who understands the significance of all stages of report production will check what has been typed and will query anything which appears to be incorrect: not the technical content (or only in exceptional circumstances), but the same name spelt in two different ways, the inconsistent abbreviation, or the omitted number in the sequence of the notation.

Nevertheless, the ultimate responsibility for the accuracy of the report belongs to the writer. He is also inevitably the most inefficient person in checking for typing errors. We all see what we know we have written, whether or not it is in front of us on the page. It is always better to ask a friend or colleague (the latter perhaps on an exchange basis) to undertake this stage of the checking, although the author can usefully check another copy at the same time. This usually results in amazement on the author's part at the number of errors which his colleague has found!

In spite of all that has been written above, the writers of reports often have to check their own work, and often do so under unrealistic time constraints. If the writing can be left alone for 48 hours, the checking will be more thorough than it would be if carried out sooner. This is the time-lag which seems to allow a writer to forget the exact words used, and therefore to look at what is on the page rather than to try to remember it. The accuracy of checking increases with the length of time-lag, and a report left for a week can be checked reasonably well by its author. A week is rarely available, and even 48 hours appears often to be a luxury.

There are, however, some guidelines for checking one's own work. Perhaps the most important is that concentration while checking does not last long: half an hour spent on checking is reasonable, while two hours is not. Even a short break after the half-hour will improve concentration when work is resumed. Within the half-hour, it is helpful both to concentration and to the avoidance of eye-strain if the focal length of viewing is changed. Simply re-focusing the eyes for a moment on the most distant object available, before returning to the checking process, is useful.

Most writers are fascinated by their own work, and it is easy to be distracted by the brilliance of the sentence further down the page and so to forget the error-filled lines which come first. Covering all of the page below the line which is being checked, and revealing the text one line at a time, slows down the reading, usefully, and ensures concentration on each line in turn. A ruler is too narrow for this, but a blank sheet of paper moved slowly down the page is a satisfactory alternative. Numbers may be checked one at a time, left to right, in the same way. Sets of figures (financial or statistical data, for example) are better checked by two people working together, one reading the figures while the other checks the page. This device should not, however, be used for the written text, as one or other of the two will usually lose concentration without the fact being obvious to the partner. 'Please would you go through the last paragraph again as I didn't notice what you said' is not a request likely to make future working relationships cordial.

It has been assumed so far that checking consists of looking for a wrong word. Much more is involved, not least the need to check the *whole* text, title page, appendices, diagrams included. The title page is often taken for granted, and the mis-spelling of the author's name, or the name of his company, is not unknown. Diagrams should be checked in the two ways suggested earlier: for technical accuracy and for errors in production. A large table of scientific data, recently seen, had probably been checked carefully several times; the two typing errors in the heading of the table inevitably made every figure suspect. The clarity of labels on diagrams has been discussed elsewhere (Chapter 5); checking clarity is important. Many typing errors are indistinguishable from spelling mistakes, except for surprises like 'cassetts' in a report from an electronics company, or 'corosion' from an engineering report. Even more surprising is the following excerpt:

Items 7, 10 and 11 were requested on 10/8/80 and were delivered with the rest of the order on the 7/7/80.

Clearly, the company concerned should flourish, with such foreknowledge of its clients' needs: unfortunately, the 7/7 should have been 7/9 (an ambiguous form of date in any case; 7 September would have been less liable to both misunderstanding and typing error). Some errors do not produce another word, or even a mis-spelt word. The same word repeated at the same point of the line, on consecutive lines, looks odd on the page. Usually a re-arrangement of the sentence (or Roget's *Thesaurus*), will solve the problem. Words or letters can be accidentally repeated, especially at a page turnover, or divided at an awkward point (the most notorious example of this is probably the incorrect division of 'therapist'). The importance of such oddities on the page is not primarily one of loss of meaning, but of loss of confidence. The reader, however favourably inclined to the material of the report, begins to doubt the information he is reading if its appearance suggests a careless approach.

Consistency

The same problem of reader goodwill makes consistency important. It does not matter whether U.S.A. appears in this form or as USA, but it matters to the reader if the usage is inconsistent. In the case of a published report, the copy-editor will tidy up such details, but for the vast number of typed reports, it has to be the job of the writer. When alternative forms of a word or abbreviation are possible, the report must be consistent in order to impress. Editorial decisions may be part of company policy, but when options exist, the writer must make a choice and then stick to it.

Copies of the text

So, finally, the report is completed, revised and thoroughly checked. The next stage will often be duplication, frequently by photocopying. There should be no difficulty with a photocopied report, provided that the original was clearly set out and typed, but even this stage can go wrong. A report with clearly numbered pages (full marks!) ran into trouble when it was found that the photocopies had pages numbered 1 to 6, 7, 7, and 9 onwards. The photocopier (human or machine) had obviously dozed off. Pages can be moved, so that they appear with the text sloping, or partly missing, or blank... the possibilities are endless. It seems churlish, after so much careful checking, to ask that the pages are collated by hand, but a random sample check might reveal a problem which affects a number of copies.

Binding

Some reports are stapled, some put into ring binders, or spiral binding, or various forms of book binding, according to their length, their importance and their distribution. The writer often has little say in this stage, but he is entitled to complain if there are too many pages for the binding, so that it splits, or if the binding chosen will not stand up to the heavy use to which the report is put. Reports used under heavy industrial conditions might need to be prepared on grease-resistant paper, with covers that can be wiped clean, but such requirements are not common. What the writer of reports should ask for is that his report, the result of so much hard work, will look good enough to create the reader response he has been hoping for since the project began.

CHAPTER 7

Specimen report

This chapter consists of the making of a report, from the initial problem to the final document as it will be distributed. As far as possible we have followed, stage by stage, the problems which might confront the report writer, and have shown how these problems can be tackled. Although the order of events is thus chronological, we have also indicated the way in which the preliminary organization will be modified as the work proceeds. The company, its problems and its reports are entirely fictitious.

Background

The Head Office of JAE Foods Ltd is in a large office block on an industrial estate on the outskirts of Basingstoke. About 300 personnel work at Head Office, and facilities appear to be good: a subsidized canteen for all staff, a licensed dining room for senior managers and visitors, and vending machines on each floor, dispensing hot and cold drinks. About a year ago, flexitime working was introduced; this was welcomed and is operating successfully.

Problem

Recently, the Catering Officer has reported a change in usage of the canteen. The number of meals served is falling, and so is the income. The Canteen Manager, who reports directly to the Catering Officer, agrees that while he has maintained a high standard of food, the financial position of the canteen is beginning to cause alarm. These comments have been brought to the attention of the Managing Director, who asks the Catering Officer to supply her with a report on the staffing and cost of both canteen and dining room. At the same time, she asks one of the Personnel staff, assisted by the Personnel Manager's secretary, to produce a second report which investigates possible changes in staff eating habits, with conclusions and/or recommendations as appropriate. (It is the latter report which is the subject of this chapter. Personnel agreement and union support have, it is assumed, been obtained.)

This is the problem as it is put to Jill Miles, Personnel Officer. She prepares her Terms of Reference and tries to write out the objective of the report very briefly, in order to clarify her own ideas and to introduce the report.

<u>Terms of Reference</u>
As Personnel Officer for JAE Foods Ltd, I have been asked by
Frances Leighton, Managing Director, to report on the reasons for the
decline in canteen usage, considering the implications of current staff
eating habits and recommending changes in catering provision which
might prove helpful to the staff. A parallel report by Philip Jenkins,
Catering Officer, will consider staffing and financial implications.
Both reports will be available to Mrs Leighton by the end of February,
1987.
<u>Objective</u>
Why are fewer people eating in the canteen, and where are they
eating instead? Can we get them back?

Jill has clearly discussed her report with her senior managers in order to clarify
exactly what she is to investigate. She has picked up the comment that 'we
must try to provide what's best for the staff, to keep up morale apart from
anything else', and she has checked on the time available to her (about three
weeks). The Terms of Reference will appear in the final report; the Objective is Jill's own—hence the informal language.

Procedure

Having made sure that she understands her brief, Jill decides on the procedure which she and Mary, the Personnel Manager's secretary, will have
to follow in order to obtain the information on which to base the report.
They decide that it would be useful to produce a questionnaire, which would
be distributed to all staff. Bearing in mind the difficulty of persuading people
to complete and return questionnaires, Jill decides to delegate one person
in each open-plan office to ask the questions directly of each staff member,
recording the answers on the prepared sheet. The process should not take
more than three or four minutes in each case, and the questions must therefore
be short and few in number. Mary agrees to organize the questionnaire
distribution and to collate the replies. Jill and Mary then prepare the questionnaire; only the analysis of replies is important to the body of the report,
but a copy of the questionnaire itself is of use to the reader, and it will
therefore become: <u>Appendix A. Questionnaire.</u>

While Mary works on the questionnaire distribution, Jill needs to find
out the comparative figures for hot and cold canteen meals over the past
year, and to check on canteen opening times. She will also look briefly at
the figures for dining room usage, in case they have any bearing on the question, and will find out whether the vending machines are providing more
or fewer cups of coffee, tea, etc., than in the past. Personal observation is
also important: Jill will talk to the canteen manager, and ask a random selec-
tion of employees for their comments; she and Mary will use the canteen,
but at different times, each day for a week.

The information generated by all this procedure will be the main body
of the report. However, Jill decides that the procedure itself deserves to be

recorded, as it will identify for the reader the basis of the findings. (Note that if Jill or Mary had consulted documents, previous reports, or articles, for instance, they would at this stage have started to compile a set of references or a bibliography.)

Procedure
1. A short questionnaire (see Appendix A) was presented to all available members of staff, and their replies were recorded.
2. Interviews were held informally with:
   Canteen Manager (Miss S. Hyde)
   Catering Officer (Mr P. Jenkins)
   15 members of staff (5% of the total, selected at random)
3. Mary Pringle and I used the canteen each working day for a week, and recorded our own observations.

As Jill and Mary proceed with their enquiries, they discover a new factor. A snacks and sandwich bar has opened a few hundred yards from JAE Foods Ltd Head Office, and the owners have started delivering sandwiches at pre-arranged times to a number of office blocks in the area. This service is proving highly popular, and groups of staff in several offices now combine to telephone an order for sausage rolls and sandwiches, which are delivered at specified times during the day. Deliveries are available from 11 a.m. to 4 p.m., provided that the order is received by 10 a.m. As the canteen has an area reserved for personnel who bring their own food, Mary takes particular note of its usage: it is often crowded. There is, incidentally, no rule against staff eating or drinking at their desks, except in a few restricted areas where there are computers.

Jill can already see a pattern to her investigation, and she draws the base (Figure 7.1) for the spider diagram on which she will gather all her information.

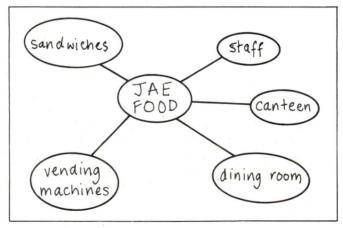

Figure 7.1 *Spider base*

78

As the reactions from interviews and questionnaires arrive, the information will be added to the appropriate 'bubble'. Staff reaction will be a constant factor, but the other 'bubbles' on the spider base will probably produce headings from which Jill can form her contents list. For the moment, she finds her material in a random way, but the following information is of note:

1. The canteen, which is self-service, is open from 12.30 to 2.15.
2. The dining room is available for evening functions. Its use, day and evening, has not changed significantly during the past year.
3. The canteen is serving fewer hot meals than in previous years; the trend seems to be steadily downwards.
4. The vending machines are heavily used: tea, coffee and squash sales are all substantially up on previous years.
5. Queues in the canteen are small, except at 12.30 when the canteen opens.

The questionnaire produced 180 replies. Staff reported that the canteen food was of good quality and reasonable in price, but there were many complaints from staff who chose to start work early, that they were hungry before 12.30. Eight staff requested that the canteen be open in the late afternoon for high tea. Many staff said that they preferred to order sandwiches, as this enabled them to save time over lunch and, because of flexitime, to finish early or 'save up' time off for an extra half-day. The vending machines were popular, but there were complaints that they were sometimes empty and that at mid-morning and mid-afternoon there were queues for the machines.

In the face of all this information, and a great deal of related detail, Jill decides that much more organization is needed before she can start to write her report. She goes back to her spider base, and adds each piece of information, noting it as a key word or phrase only (the original information can be looked up during the actual writing). First, she deals with Mary's analysis of the questionnaire replies, adding information to appropriate 'bubbles'; then she adds the results of interviews, and lastly her own and Mary's observations. The spider is now complete (see Figure 7.2 on page 80).

The advantage to Jill of using the spider is that each piece of information in turn can be added to the appropriate place (and subsequently moved if necessary). Had she listed points under the same headings, she would have had to scan the questionnaire responses for information concerning the canteen, then scan the manager's comments for information about the canteen, and then look for related information in her own and Mary's notes. The whole process of scanning would then be repeated for the vending machines, and then for the dining room, and then for the sandwich bar: a very cumbersome and time-consuming process. From the spider format, it is comparatively easy to draw conclusions and to see connections; for example, the link between flexitime and the desire for earlier canteen opening.

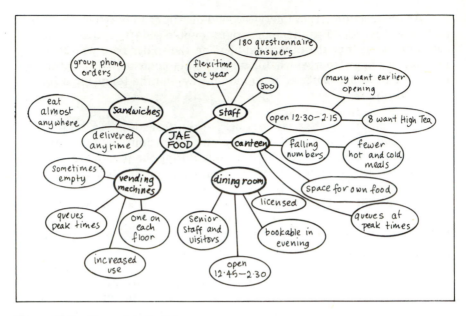

Nodes in the spider diagram:

- **JAE FOOD** (center)
  - **Sandwiches**
    - group phone orders
    - eat almost anywhere
    - delivered any time
  - **staff**
    - flexitime one year
    - 180 questionnaire answers
    - 300
  - **canteen**
    - open 12·30 – 2·15
    - many want earlier opening
    - 8 want High Tea
    - falling numbers
    - fewer hot and cold meals
  - **vending machines**
    - sometimes empty
    - queues peak times
    - one on each floor
    - increased use
  - **dining room**
    - Senior Staff and visitors
    - open 12·45 – 2·30
    - bookable in evening
    - licensed
    - space for own food
    - queues at peak times

Figure 7.2 *Completed spider*

The contents list which began with the spider base diagram can now be drawn up in detail, and Jill does this:

Sections 7 and 8 might need sub-division, but it is difficult to be sure at this stage. Jill can, however, now start writing her report, and she will most probably start with section 3, 4, 5 or 6: it does not matter which. The language she uses is, of course, formal, but since the report will be seen only by the staff of JAE Foods Ltd, she is allowed to use the first person ('I observed that...'), and she does so. One section of the main body of the report reads as follows:

3. CANTEEN
    The self-service canteen is open on Monday to Friday from 12.30 to 2.15. There is seating for 95 people, including some tables reserved for staff who bring their own food.
    3.1 Staff Responses
         It was generally agreed that the quality of the food was good and the subsidized price reasonable.
         The question of hours of opening produced the following comments:
         (1) Staff who begin work at 8.00 would like the canteen to be open for lunch before 12.30.
         (2) Eight members of staff who frequently work in the evening would like the canteen to serve high tea in the late afternoon.
         (3) Many staff complained that queues at 12.30 meant a long wait (up to 10 minutes) before they could serve their food. An earlier start, it was suggested, would ease the queue problem.
    3.2 Interview with Canteen Manager
         The Canteen Manager reported that the number of hot and cold meals served had decreased steadily over the previous eight months.
         Nevertheless, she was aware that queues formed just before 12.30, and that those who arrived at exactly 12.30 sometimes had to wait up to 10 minutes before reaching the self-service area.
    3.3 Observations
         Visits by the report writers to the canteen suggested that queues were rare, except at 12.30, when they seemed to build up quickly.
         The canteen area reserved for staff who brought their own food was full on several occasions during the week of observation (16-20 February 1987).

On the basis of this evidence and that of the rest of the report, Jill can come to specific conclusions. She will not at this point suggest what action should be taken, nor will she introduce any new evidence. Part of the conclusions section is given below.

7. CONCLUSIONS
   (1) The canteen is used less than in the past, apart from the area reserved for those who bring their own food.
   (2) Staff are dissatisfied with the present opening hours of the canteen, especially since the introduction of flexitime.
   (3) Many staff order sandwiches, to be delivered at any convenient time during the day, from the sandwich bar.
   (4) Use of the vending machines has increased rapidly during the past year.
   (5) Use of the dining room has shown no significant change.

It is helpful to list the conclusions in this way, as many readers will find this section and the recommendations particularly useful. In this case, the Managing Director may read only these parts of the report. Jill can be subjective in her recommendations, provided that all she recommends is firmly based on the evidence presented. This will be the next section of the report to be written.

8. RECOMMENDATIONS
   In the light of the above conclusions, I recommend that consideration be given to extending the opening hours of the canteen at lunch time, preferably by allowing lunch to be served from 12.00 onwards.
   There is insufficient demand to warrant opening the canteen at any time other than at lunchtime.
   Vending machines are heavily used, and I recommend that more be provided, perhaps two on each floor instead of the present one.
   The provision of sandwiches is obviously very popular, especially as they can be eaten at any time during the working day. I suggest that the possibility of our own canteen supplying sandwiches, perhaps for an hour before lunch, be investigated. Sandwiches might be ordered on the previous day, and delivered to each department in the morning, if demand is sufficient. The current use of the sandwich bar suggests that this would be an additional service welcomed by the staff.

The report is now well on its way to completion. As it seems likely that copies will be circulated to all senior staff, Jill considers the need for a summary. The report is not long (perhaps five or six pages in all), but a summary will emphasize her conclusions and recommendations, and will be useful in reminding her readers of the subject of the report. On balance, she decides that it is worth writing a very short summary, as an *aide-mémoire* and for those who will never find time to read the whole report. Jill sets herself a limit of 100 words. Her first version covers the ideas adequately, but is too long:

SUMMARY

This report <u>investigates</u> the recent decline in the use of the canteen, and <u>considers</u> other means of food and drink provision ~~for staff at~~ Head Office. Investigation shows that since the introduction of flexitime, staff need ~~lunch earlier than allowed by the 12.30 opening~~ *extended lunch time opening*. ~~Indeed~~, many prefer to order sandwiches from a local ~~sandwich bar~~ *source* ~~rather than eat in the canteen~~. They ~~then~~ *therefore* buy ~~hot-or-cold~~ drinks from the vending machines, which are over-used ~~as a result~~.
~~The report therefore~~ *I* recommends that lunchtime opening hours for the canteen are extended, ~~and that~~ *with* the possibility of the canteen itself serving sandwiches. ~~should be investigated.~~ ~~A greater number of~~ *More* vending machines are *urgently* needed.

(114 words)

Jill has cut out unnecessary words ('therefore' instead of 'as a result'), and omitted unnecessary detail (the opening time of the canteen, for instance). She tidies up her style ('investigates' and 'Investigation' at the beginning), and stresses the urgency of extra vending machines, as this can probably be implemented while the other suggestions are being discussed, a move which will raise staff morale. Her final version is well within her word limit:

SUMMARY
In this report, I have considered food and drink provision for Head Office personnel, and investigated the reasons for the decline in use of the canteen.
Since the introduction of flexitime, many staff find the canteen opening hours too restricted, prefer to order sandwiches from an outside source, and buy drinks from the over-used vending machines in the Head Office building.
Extended lunchtime opening hours for the canteen are recommended, with the possibility of the canteen itself serving sandwiches.
Additional vending machines are urgently needed.

(85 words)

Mary will now type the report, adding a simple title page:

JAE FOODS LTD
Maple Drive
Basingstoke, Hampshire

REPORT ON THE PROVISION OF FOOD AND DRINK
FOR HEAD OFFICE STAFF

JILL MILES
25 February, 1987

The contents list will follow the title page, then the summary, and then the full report with its pages numbered. As there are no references or bibliography, the report will conclude with Appendix A (the questionnaire). It is now Jill's responsibility to check the report and the typing (although Mary will have done this already), and she has wisely left herself a couple of days in which to do this. Her name and the date are already on the title page, but she may feel that she should also sign the document personally, at the end of the text but before the appendix. As the report will have a small, internal circulation, the pages may simply be stapled together, or put in a plain plastic cover. Photocopies will be made, if necessary, before the stapling is done!

Jill Miles is pleased with her report, but the final judgement will be that of her Managing Director. If the recommendations form a useful basis for further discussion, the report can be considered a success.

Case studies

Introduction

The following ten case studies, except for the visit report, are based on real-life information, although names of people, companies, products and, in one case, countries, have all been changed to preserve confidentiality. Any resemblance to existing names is coincidental.

The first three case studies, an accident report, laboratory report and visit report, are 'specialized', in that they require a particular organization of material, and headings which are different from those of general advisory reports (see Chapter 3). Each of case studies 4 to 7 provides the basis for a complete report, although the student might feel that extra appropriate information could be added (Case study 8 J.S. Morgan Ltd, is always in this category). This is a matter for discussion whenever the case studies are used. The final two case studies involve the writing of sections of reports rather than complete documents. Lecturers or seminar leaders might wish to add further technical information to develop these into full reports.

The case studies can all be used as individual exercises, but some lend themselves particularly well to small group work (the Huntsford report and Cotham House are in this category). It is advisable to allow plenty of time for the case studies: a minimum recommended time allowance is given with the notes to individual studies. There are, of course, no single 'right answers' to such exercises, but guidance in using each case study is given in the notes.

Tutors and students should work through the main text of the book together before attempting this work.

Case study 1   Accident report

Note

As the information given below indicates, the material for this case study is presented as informal notes written by a driver involved in a motorway pile-up. In this type of report, emphasis will be on relevance and objectivity. Some information, such as the date and time of the accident, must always be given, while other information, such as weather conditions, is helpful and easily verifiable from other sources.

The writer must not 'colour' his report to the police: while it is written from his viewpoint (the facts as he saw them), he must try to be impartial and to avoid guesswork. The finished document will be as short as possible, without conclusions or recommendations, but, as are all reports, signed and dated (this date being the date of the report as opposed to the date of the accident).

Minimum time allowed: 30 minutes

Background

The accident recorded below took place on a motorway in extremely poor driving conditions. The information is given from the point of view of Andrew Carter, one of the drivers involved; realizing that he would have to give statements to his insurance company and to the police, he sat down on the day after the accident and noted everything that he could remember which might be useful in making a statement. Later, the police asked him for a written record of the events leading to the accident and its immediate aftermath. He used the following notes to help him with his report.

1. The accident was just before Christmas, 23 December. I was driving north up the M1, bringing my mother and sister to our house for the holiday. They were with me in the car.

2. It was a dreadful day, gloomy, damp, intermittent drizzle.

3. There was a great deal of traffic, including some lunatic driving we'd seen earlier, and we were all a bit nervous. The motorway was very congested.

4. I was driving my Polo Classic, two years old, but I'd had it only four months. 18 000 miles on the clock.

5. I think there was an accident somewhere ahead. I couldn't see it, but judging by the traffic conditions and by what people said, there seemed to have been a collision of some sort about a quarter of a mile in front, just a few minutes earlier.

6. It was about 3 o'clock in the afternoon. I had my dipped headlights on because of poor visibility. Quite a lot of cars had their lights on.

7. We were in the outside lane, but all three lanes were very full and we couldn't have got to the 70 mph limit if we'd wanted to. We were travelling at about 50 mph when our accident happened.

86

8. It was hard to keep enough distance between cars. I held back from the car in front, and had the impression that the driver behind was keeping his distance, too. The middle lane was moving even more slowly, and the cars were catching up on one another. The inner lane seemed to be crowded, as far as I could see.

9. We were in Northamptonshire. We stopped near Post 128/3. I noticed that later.

10. The accident ahead, the one I couldn't see, seemed to result in another collision, only four or five cars ahead of us. I saw brake-lights going on, and I braked fairly gently at first.

11. One of the cars ahead, the fourth from us, a Cortina, spun round and finished up blocking the outside and middle lanes at right angles to the flow of traffic. The cars immediately in front and behind it looked badly damaged, and I suppose they all collided.

12. All I could be sure of was that the car in front of me, the Maestro, went into a skid and ended up half on the central reservation. I braked sharply then, and came to a complete stop, just short of the Maestro.

13. The cars in the middle lane stopped. One of them skidded and stopped close to the car behind the Cortina, but I don't know whether it ran into the Cortina or not.

14. My mother, who was in the front passenger seat, exclaimed something, 'Look out!' or something like that, and I think I said, 'It's all right'. She leant forward to brace herself in case we hit the Maestro, but we didn't, and I could see we weren't going to hit it.

15. Almost immediately afterwards, there was an almighty bang, and the car behind us, the old Escort driven by Mr David Jones, hit us with considerable force. I didn't think he was so close; he must have been slow in reacting, or perhaps his brakes weren't very good.

16. My mother screamed (she's elderly and nervous anyway), and she hit her head hard against the headrest. Thank goodness I've got them, and we all had our safety belts on, of course.

17. When it was safe and the other cars moved, at least those that could, I pulled across to the hard shoulder and was exchanging details with Mr Jones, the Escort driver, when the police arrived. We gave them some of this information.

18. I've driven for 20 years, and had only two accidents, one soon after I started driving and one about seven or eight years ago. It wasn't my fault and I didn't lose my no claims bonus.

19. The ambulance arrived, and one of the ambulance men thought my mother ought to have a check-up at the hospital. In fact, she had badly bruised and strained neck and shoulder muscles, but nothing worse. My sister and I were not hurt. Anne, my sister, saw a good deal of what happened round about us, as she was sitting at the back. Nobody in Mr Jones' car seemed to be hurt, but the ambulance men took away several people from the Cortina and the cars round it.

20. I didn't skid at all when I stopped. I remember being pleased about that.

21. Eventually I was able to drive on slowly, when the police said I could, and I collected my mother from the hospital. The back of my car was a mess, rear bumper, rear lights, bootlid all damaged, but the car drove all right, except for odd noises at the back.
22. I'm a school teacher, 43 years old. I drive quite a lot, to school 15 miles away, and socially and so on.
23. The police didn't see the accident, but they might have seen the first one, ahead. They arrived very quickly.
24. The car behind the Escort was touching the Escort when it stopped, but as far as I could see there was no damage.

Case study 2 Laboratory report

Note

This is a specialized report containing technical information, and probably of use only to pure science students. A piece of equipment, a spectrophotometer, is evaluated (details of the manufacturer have been omitted and the figures changed slightly to preserve confidentiality).

At present, the information given is badly organized, and it would be difficult to base a decision about purchase or usage on such confused material. It should be rewritten in a logical way, with formal English usage, in order that a proper assessment can be made. The headings will closely follow those suggested in Chapter 3, for laboratory reports, with a brief conclusion about the suitability of the equipment for laboratory use.

Minimum time allowed: 1 hour

Evaluation of the new spectrophotometer

This new spectrophotometer is a standard spectrophotometer using a tungsten light source, diffraction grating monochromator and a linear absorbance photometer. It has a spectral range from 330–750 nm and an absorbance range from 0–3A. There is a rapid sampling cuvette adaptor available for this spectrophotometer.

The manufacturer recommends a minimum sample volume of 0.25 ml. The instrument specification states that long-term stability should be less than 0.004A. The manufacturer also states that a carryover of less than 1% should be obtained using a purge time of 3 seconds.

A test was carried out to check the minimum sample volume. The aspiration time was varied from 0.1 seconds to 1.0 seconds in 0.1 second intervals; and the vacuum was reduced from 16 to 4 inches of mercury in 1 inch intervals. The first sample was of distilled water which was weighed before and after aspiration. It was found that with a minimum sample time of 0.1 seconds and a vacuum of 4 inches of mercury, the volume required was 0.16 ml. Such a reduction in volume could well affect carryover. The manufacturer's minimum sample volume of 0.25 ml was found to be achievable using an aspiration time of 0.1 seconds.

The second sample was of a reagent with a specific gravity greater than one. A vacuum of 14 inches of mercury was required, but whatever the aspiration time, the sample volume remained 0.25 ml. Aspiration continued after the aspiration valve had closed. Clearly, this was less satisfactory than with the aqueous solution. Great care was needed in the setting of the vacuum.

In practice a carryover of less than 1% was achieved with a purge time of 0.4 seconds. Although it is unlikely that such a short time would be used. This sample to sample carryover was determined for purge times of between 0.1 and 1.0 seconds, in the usual way by reading alternating groups of three specimens. The first group was a solution, absorbance approx. 1.8A, and the other group water tests. At 0.1 seconds the carryover value was 0.0314 and this fell to 0.0013 at 1.0 seconds. Therefore, in the routine situation it is unlikely that purge time would affect carryover.

The stability of the absorbance value also fell within the specification. Experiments produced a standard deviation of ±0.0012 giving a range of 0.0038. This was assessed by using a potassium permanganate solution (max. absorbance 615nm) with readings being taken every 10 seconds. 25 readings gave a mean value of 1.093A.

Case study 3   Visit report

Note

It would be impossible to use a 'real-life' visit report as a case study, but the authors of this book have seen many such reports, and have frequently been amazed at the irrelevant 'chatter' which is included. The case study is a slightly exaggerated version of an amalgam of such reports.

A visit report is sometimes produced on a company pro forma, and some details, such as name and address of company visited, date, reason for and outcome of the visit, are essential. So, frequently, is information about action which needs to be taken. Other material is helpful, such as brief details of arrangements which might be of use in planning future visits. Subjective views of the company visited may be included, but only if it is clear that these are opinions not facts, and only if the whole report is classified as confidential. Occasionally, information about the country and its political or economic structure might be included, but only if it is relevant to the project under discussion. Personal details of expenses and the like should be itemized elsewhere.

From the material given in this case study, the student must select what is appropriate to a visit report, and organize it clearly and concisely.
Minimum time allowed: 1 hour

Geoffrey's report
Report on visit to the Redillione factory in Tyrolingia on the 2nd July–5th July 1996 to see Josef Sbriginski and Georg Mende about the new TLA system with a view to using this equipment at our new Wrighton factory.

Acknowledgements
May I say how grateful I am to Josef Sbriginski and Georg Mende for all the time and trouble they took to look after me and to Jean, my secretary, for arranging my flights and hotel accommodation, and, of course, to my dear wife for so helpfully driving me to and from the airport in England.

Contents
1. Introduction   00
2. Meeting   00
3. Recommendations   00

1. Introduction
   Tyrolingia is a vast country, full of copses and pleasant meadows and it is a lovely place to visit. It has a population of 22 million, many of whom seem to be employed in the tourist and catering trades. My atlas tells me that Tyrolingia has an area of 548 000 km^2 and its people's main language is Tyrolingo. However, most of the people I met spoke fairly

fluent English and, other than a slight problem one morning in the newspaper shop, I had no difficulty either in understanding them or in making myself understood.

2. Meeting

Originally, it was planned that I should be met at the airport by someone from Redillione, but that plan misfired. However, a young lady called Anna kindly did a lot of ringing around for me and arranged a hire car. Unfortunately, my wallet containing my driving licence was right at the bottom of my suitcase and they wanted to see it before handing me the car. I paid for the car with my own credit card, so I will have to submit a separate expenses claim for that. My other expenses are all on the pink form, which Dave authorized.

A night in the Hotel Nesting, during which I slept very little. The hotel was noisy, I think it was someone's birthday because the disco music was still playing at 2 a.m. I would not recommend that this is used by other staff. The bed was too narrow and the food was very greasy and not too warm. Anyway, in the morning I drove to Redillione. I have driven on the right before on holiday, but never in a left-hand drive car. It was quite an experience. Redillione is in the midst of some really beautiful countryside. It was worth the drive along the muddy, pot-holed track to see the views.

I was greeted by Josef and Georg. They were really great. I was treated more like a close friend than a business customer. Nothing was too much trouble; they gave me coffee and took me to a lovely local restaurant for lunch where we had grilled Steppe viper which they explained was the local speciality. If anyone else goes to visit do see me first and I will give you the name of the restaurant. After all their generous hospitality it seems a bit off for me to say, but I feel that I must, that despite their assurances that Redillione was a professional company the fact that (a) J.S. and G.M. did not wear suits (b) many offices were stacked high with papers and (c) the car park was full of wrecks, indicated that this may not be the case.

The plan was that I arrived in Tyrolingia on the 2nd in the evening and then on the 3rd I would spend the morning having meetings with the guys who wrote the spec for the TLA system and in the afternoon I would be taken to Lialinde where the TLA system is installed and working. Last time I travelled abroad I claimed my expenses on the pink form and even though it was immediately approved, I did not receive any money until three months later, by which time my bank manager was breathing down my neck. I think that if the company expects its personnel to go abroad then this system of payment had better be improved. Anyway, after that experience I thought I deserved to take the 4th July as a holiday and remain in the hotel, and then fly home on the 5th. As it turned out, however, the system at Lialinde had gone down and so Redillione's engineers had had to go to Lialinde to try and sort out the problem. This left me with Josef and Georg in the morning. Unfortunately, they did not know the detailed specification of the system and the best they could do was to give me the manuals. Some of the details in these seem to have lost something in translation. Anyway, the specs have been passed on to Mike and he and I will analyse them in due course. Because of the problem, I was unable to visit the site where the system is—or as it so happened is not—in operation.

All in all the day was very frustrating and left me feeling so down that my day off was also pretty much a waste of time. I was quite relieved when the plane landed in England and I knew I was safely home again.

3. ## Recommendations

I would certainly recommend that anyone who can spare the time should visit Tyrolingia, and see for themselves what a superb country it is. I would like to express my thanks to my boss (Dave) for allowing me to visit such a delightful place.

As to Redillione, well I am not so impressed. Their trading record needs to be established. I would recommend that recommendations from their current customers are obtained.

The new TLA system apparently has many bugs, although Redillione did assure me that all the major problems have been sorted out and it is only minor ones that remain. I would recommend that the system manuals are carefully examined and if both these and Redillione's track record are satisfactory then a further visit to see the system in operation should be implemented.

Case study 4   Garage report

Note

This case study is based on a real incident, but for obvious reasons the make of car has been disguised and a non-existent registration number given.

The task is to select information which is useful in a permanent record made in case of future queries, and to reject material which involves personalities or which is irrelevant to the facts of the case. The information can be presented in either of two ways: as recommended, in the form of a short memo and accompanying pro forma, or as a short report incorporating the technical details.

Minimum time allowed: 30 minutes

Record of events

In the autumn of 1985, work was carried out at the County Garages Ltd workshops on a Zedmobile, registration number MJV 369Z. The car is not a make appropriate to the franchise, and was not acquired as part of a trade-in deal. After a query from the area manager on a routine visit, the County Garages Service Manager, Jim Phillips, decided that a record should be kept of the unusual circumstances under which the car came in. He therefore prepared a short report in the form of a memo, to which he attached the pro forma on which service details are recorded.

The following information was available to him.

A friend of Alan Collinson, the General Manager, owned the Zedmobile, having acquired it on the death of his father. As he had no use for it himself, he approached Alan and asked him to sell it, getting as good a price as was reasonable. Alan agreed, and enquired from several of his usual dealers what they would be willing to give to take the car off his hands. The best offer was from Ted Finch, a dealer in Manchester, about 40 miles away. The offer was provisionally accepted, on a 'sold as seen with all known faults declared' basis. As far as Alan knew, there were no problems with the car, which appeared to have been well maintained, and when Ted saw the car, he was happy to buy it.

Ted took the car with him straight away, and was eight miles down the M6 when he saw the oil-pressure gauge falling rapidly and heard strange noises from the engine compartment; this caused him to pull off onto the hard shoulder and telephone for help. The car was towed back to County Garages, where Ted told Alan in no uncertain terms his opinion of the car and of the deal. Alan, who was anxious to continue to do business with Ted, asked his Service Manager, Jim, to find out what had gone wrong and why. Jim started up the engine, heard the noise and diagnosed big end failure.

Alan contacted his friend, the previous owner, and together with Ted, now the legal owner, discussed the situation. It was agreed that County Garages should remove the engine and repair it at minimum cost, that is, deal with the big end failure and nothing more. Jim was, however, asked to report on why the engine should have failed so soon after the handover. He had the engine stripped down and examined. The mechanic noticed that the oil was heavily contaminated. However, as there was no heat damage to the con-rod, the only repair which seemed necessary was to have the crankshaft re-ground and rebuilt, with new bearings.

Jim considered the possibility that the previous owner of the vehicle had 'tidied up' the engine sufficiently to allow it to run for a short distance with no obvious signs of trouble, but on the whole he was inclined to discount this. Alan's friend was a regular customer, and had a good relationship with the garage staff, in addition to his long-standing friendship with Alan (they had been at college together). It seemed more likely that the owner's father, who had been in poor health for several years before his death, had used the car for short runs only and had had it serviced on a mileage basis rather than every six months. The oil would, therefore, have remained unchanged for a longer time than was recommended. A short run at what, for this car, was unusually high speed, had uncovered the problem. Alan's friend was inclined to agree that his father might have driven the car slowly and for only short distances.

There remained the question of the bill for the repair. Alan was anxious to get the car off the premises, as he had serious problems of space; his friend was embarrassed by what had happened but anxious to keep what he felt was a good price for the car, and the dealer wanted to sell the car quickly and recover any loss he might make as a result of the repair. They agreed amicably to divide the bill equally between them, and the dealer added his share of the bill to the price of the car. He sold it soon afterwards, and the incident was officially closed, but recorded in case of any future query.

Case study 5   The Fosbury Problem

Note

At present, this case study is in the form of an essay. The style and expression are acceptable, but the essay will need drastic re-organization into report form.

    The terms of reference for the report call for a formal document to be given to the Huntsford licensing magistrates, to persuade them that the quality of life in the Fosbury Precinct would deteriorate further if certain licences were granted. Some of the information contained in the essay is irrelevant to these terms of reference, but extra material (for instance, about the records of the local police) could be added by the student.

    This case study is particularly suitable for students who need to identify and practise the differing skills needed for essays and reports, and especially, in the latter, the use of short, precise headings.

Minimum time allowed: 1 hour (more if additional material is required)

Essay

Architects and town planners have long known what is 'best' for people, what kind of home anybody would welcome and live in happily ever after. People, unfortunately, do not always conform to official planning, and building techniques are not always capable of withstanding the structural pressures put upon them. Good ideas, for example the linking in a pedestrian precinct of shops and accommodation, sometimes result in problems unforeseen by the planners.

    Such a problem is presented by the Fosbury Precinct, in the new town of Huntsford. Huntsford itself grew rapidly for about 20 years, particularly after the arrival of a number of light engineering companies, but its size steadied at about 47 500 acres and its population at about 150 000. A number of large estates were built in the 1960s; these now tend to house a high proportion of teenagers and of elderly people living alone. There are a few more recent developments, among them the Fosbury Precinct, an attempt to join a pedestrian shopping area with accommodation in the form of 40 flats.

    The Fosbury Precinct is built on two levels, joined by two long, spiralling ramps and, under cover at one end, 'up' and 'down' escalators. Car parking spaces are available on the perimeter of the precinct, and these have led to vigorous dispute: it was assumed, totally erroneously, that only one flat owner in two would have a car. Spaces are reserved for residents, but on a 'first come, first served' basis, which causes resentment, not least among young people who need cars for work. The spaces are often taken, especially in the evenings, by patrons of the Taj Mahal Restaurant, and this has caused general irritation and one or two ugly incidents.

    The upper level of the precinct has a few shops (dress shop, hairdresser's, children's wear), but it is mainly composed of forty small, two-bedroomed flats, thirty-seven of which are at present occupied. The residents consist of six couples (senior citizens), four single senior citizens, ten young couples without children, nine single people, mostly in their twenties and thirties, and eight couples with small children. The total adult population is sixty-one (14 of whom are over sixty-five years of age), and the total child population is eleven (seven of whom are under five years old).

The lower level of the Fosbury Precinct contains shops (a small super-market, greengrocer's, butcher's), and also the William of Fosbury public house. This is named after a local hero of the days when Fosbury was a village, and is known to the local people as 'The William'. It has tried to keep to the best tradition of an English country pub, and is quiet, a little old-fashioned, and very popular with the older people in the district. The landlord, Bill Hinkley, is a quiet, pleasant man, a stronger character than he appears on the surface, and greatly liked and respected locally.

About three years ago, an Indian restaurant called the Taj Mahal was opened on the opposite side of the ground floor square to The William. There were complaints from the local people and from the landlord of The William, especially as the Taj Mahal was licensed until midnight, but the restaurant has been well managed and it is now at least tolerated by the residents, apart from sporadic complaints about cooking smells in hot weather. The local people eat there occasionally and it attracts custom from the neighbouring areas of Huntsford, including the nearest of the large estates.

However, vague discontent in the precinct turned into anger about eight months ago, when a disco called Jim's Joint opened; it is licensed for normal hours, and has attracted groups of teenagers from a wide area of Huntsford. Noise late at night, fighting, and broken bottles littering the precinct have roused the residents to fury; some of the shops have been vandalized, as has an empty flat, and the precinct's three telephone kiosks are now rarely operational. The last straw has been the purchase by the owner of the Taj Mahal of additional premises near his restaurant; he intends to use these as a Pizza Bar in order to attract a wider—and younger—clientele. He has already appointed a manager and is about to apply for a licence for alcohol (until 2 a.m.) and also a licence for live music. The residents, in an effort to persuade the licensing magistrates to refuse both licences, called a public meeting.

The meeting was not a success. It was chaired by a local councillor, who was torn between his concern for the elderly (for many years part of his political campaigning) and his desire to give local young people somewhere to go. Unemployment in Huntsford is above the national average and is rising; the councillor was anxious about being seen as 'against' unemployed young people. He was involved in the meeting at the request of the residents, but was clearly (perhaps too clearly) unhappy about chairing it.

Feelings at the meeting ran high: an elderly patron of The William, who remembers the old Fosbury village, spoke passionately about the effect of the noise and disturbance on the nerves of his sick wife; the father of two small children, desperate to move to more spacious accommodation but unable to afford a house, was vehemently but inarticulately concerned about the effect of vandalism and delinquency on his youngsters; a social worker, anxious about the welfare of the children, had been trying to stir the Environmental Health Officer to action, but without success. Unfortunately, the future manager of the Pizza Bar, young and self-confident, antagonized residents by his lack of understanding of their concern. He saw his new job as a breakthrough to a managerial future, and was willing to be ruthless in pursuit of his career. The Headmaster of the local primary school, although sympathetic to the parents and anxious about his children, tried to cool tempers at the meeting and failed, to his personal distress.

Realizing that public meetings were not likely to help their case, the residents formed a small committee to organize a more peaceful and effective protest. The Headmaster reluctantly agreed to organize a formal report to be handed to the licensing magistrates, setting out the residents' objections to licences for the Pizza Bar (they would like to have the licence removed from Jim's Joint if they could, but realize that this is probably beyond them at the moment). Helping the Headmaster to collect and organize the evidence are the landlord of The William (anxious not only about the effect on his own trade, but also about the shortage of car parking spaces and the noise from the Pizza Bar if it is opened), and the social worker. Between them, they talk to residents, collect evidence of increasing vandalism, discuss the situation with the local police, and produce their own reasons for opposing the Pizza Bar licences. They then meet to assemble the information gathered, and the Headmaster is asked to use this material as the basis for a report.

Case study 6 Huntsford Borough Council :
Enquiry into Licensed Premises, 1983

Note

The terms of reference for this report need careful study. The issue is to be discussed by the Borough Councillors, who will use the information at a meeting. A short, well-spaced, clearly-headed report will therefore be necessary. An indication of significant trends is requested, but no suggestion for action. Both detailed statistics and trends must be presented in such a way that neither irritation nor bewilderment results.

Minimum time allowed: 2 hours

Terms of Reference

After adverse comments in the local press about the supervision of licensed premises in the town, the Borough Council asked for comparative figures for the last full year (1982), 1980 and 1978 to be prepared as a basis for discussion.

An Administrative Officer with the Town Clerk's Department has been asked to prepare a draft report including the statistics available, drawing attention to significant trends and commenting where appropriate.

The report must be available to the Town Clerk in time for the Council meeting on Friday 13 May, 1983.

The information which is available now follows.

Huntsford has a total acreage of 45 750. The population is now approximately 150 000, representing a slight increase over the late 1970s. The town includes a number of large estates built in the 1960s, where there is now a high population of teenagers and of elderly people living alone.

Licensed Premises in Huntsford

The estimated population gives an average of 1875 people per public house. There were 80 full Publicans' Licences issued last year, the same number as for the 3 previous years, and 2 more than in 1977 or 1978. Publicans' Licences with conditions have dropped by 1 from the figure issued for the previous 5 years, which was 18. On the other hand, clubs with Justices' Licences appear to be on the increase, from 8 to 11 over the past two years, compared with 3 to 5 between 1975 and 1978.

Licensed Shops and 'Off' licensed premises have inevitably become more numerous with the growth of population: only 16 shops held licences in 1978, a figure which rose to 19 in 1980 and by 1982 stood at 21. Similarly, there has been a growth of 25 per cent in the number of 'Off' licensed premises between 1980 and 1982, and a similar growth in the preceding two years; the 1982 total was 25.

In 1978, 17 restaurant licences were issued, and 2 residential and restaurant licences. By 1980, the former had risen to 18, and by 1982 to 23. The latter figure rose to 3 in 1980, and has so far remained constant. Residential licences have remained constant at 2 each year for the last eight years.

Extensions of permitted hours are commonly granted for Bank Holidays (a total of 239 in 1982, 201 in 1978 and 228 in 1980). Other social occasions for which extensions have been granted have included a large number of dances (619), which is an increase of 18 over the 1980 figure and of 22 over the 1978 figure. The biggest increase has been in the number of extensions granted for parties,* the 158 last year being 48 more than in 1980, and 70 more than in 1978. Licences for social evenings, on the contrary, have declined, from 189 in 1978 to 183 in 1980 and 169 in the last year. The number of darts matches in the area remains reasonably constant, 12 licences being granted in 1982 as against 11 in 1980 and 9 in 1978. The rise in meetings for which extensions were granted was also small: 7 in 1982, 5 in 1980 and 4 in 1978.

Wedding receptions and dinners have both increased significantly in number, the former producing 39 applications in 1982, 37 in 1980 and 30 in 1978. The latter increased by 25 per cent from the 21 in 1978 (1980 produced 26 applications).

Naturally, a town such as Huntsford also demands a number of extensions which cannot easily be categorized. Such miscellaneous applications resulted in the granting of 74 extensions in 1978, 69 in 1980 and 80 in 1982.

*Note: 'parties' is held to include discos.

Occasional licences have, of course, been granted during the past five years, most commonly for public dances (508 in 1982, 522 in 1980 and 513 in 1978). However, the number of parties* has produced a sharp increase in the applications for occasional licences, from 48 in 1978 to an unprecedented 93 in 1982. The biggest increase has been in the last two years, from 59 to 93.

Socials and shows remain reasonably constant, the former moving from 72 in 1978 to 75 in 1980 and to 76 in 1982. The number of licences for shows was 24 in both 1980 and 1982, and 23 two years earlier.

Perhaps the success of the local Young Athletes Clubs has contributed to the number of applications from Sports Meetings—18 last year, as opposed to 14 in 1980 and only 11 in 1978.

Garden Fêtes requested and were granted 9 licences last year, as against 7 in 1980, and 6 in 1978.

General activities classified as 'Miscellaneous' produced 31 licences in 1982 and 28 in 1978**.

*Note: 'parties' is held to include discos.
** Handwritten note: I can't find the figure for 1980. For goodness' sake blur it over somehow. Thanks, Jim.

The police made a total of 1220 routine visits during normal permitted hours in 1982 (1190 in 1980, 1180 in 1978), and 111 visits to premises where permitted hours had been extended or occasional licences granted (133 in 1980, 148 in 1978).

Fourteen incidents which required police intervention were recorded in 1982, as against 6 in 1980 and only 2 in 1978. These incidents resulted in arrests in 5 cases (2 in 1980, none in 1978).

During the years under discussion, a number of persons were convicted of offences in connection with the consumption of alcohol, the most notable being the number convicted of driving a motor vehicle while having an alcohol level above the prescribed limit. There were 112 such convictions in 1978, 133 in 1980 and 210 in 1982. Fourteen people failed to provide a specimen of breath (6 in 1980, 5 in 1978) and 6 failed to provide a specimen for laboratory testing (3 in 1978, 4 in 1980).

The number of drunk and disorderly convictions also rose, from 43 in 1978 to 47 in 1980 and to 98 in 1982. Drunk and incapable convictions rose, reaching 51 in 1982, from 30 in 1980 and only 27 in 1978.

Two licencees were convicted in 1982 of selling alcohol to a person under age; there is no precedent for this. These were also 8 convictions for consuming alcohol while under age; there had been no record of such a conviction for the previous 10 years.

Of the 389 persons convicted in 1982, 340 lived locally; of the 220 convicted in 1980, 217 lived locally, and of the 190 persons convicted in 1978, 113 lived locally.

Extract from the *Huntsford Recorder*, Friday 15 April 1983

NEAR TRAGEDY AT COMMUNITY CENTRE

PANIC which might well have resulted in tragedy broke out on Wednesday evening at the local Community Centre on the Elverton Estate.

Youngsters celebrating the 18th birthday of Sally Johnson, a sixth-former at Elverton Comprehensive School, found that the fire doors were locked. Several of the teenagers screamed, and panic spread rapidly. In the rush, three of Sally's friends were hurt and needed hospital treatment, and a number of the teenagers suffered bruises and shock.

Sally's mother told our reporter, 'We'd done everything to keep the party quiet and respectable. We've no idea who locked the doors, but the kids were frightened and you can't blame them. The police said the doors should have been open, but I want to know why they weren't checked. Some people said that the kids had drunk too much and that it was a fight that broke out, but it just isn't true.' Police said afterwards that drinking hours had been extended, but there was no evidence of the youngsters drinking too much... .

Leader comment: Too often in recent months we have had to report trouble at teenage parties, often when there has been too much alcohol and too little supervision...

Case study 7 Cryptic and warning devices in butterflies and moths found in the Magna Parva area of Sussex.

Note

This is the transcript of a conversation between Professor R. Oliver, Emeritus Professor of Applied Entomology at London University, and research student Charles Turpin, visiting the Professor for the day. Professor Oliver made his retirement home in the small village of Magna Parva some five years ago, but takes a lively interest in the lepidoptera around. Charles is collecting material for his thesis and for discussion with a group of fellow students.

Topics which the two discussed included the nature of the locality, ideas of cryptic and warning colouration, and specific examples recorded locally by Professor Oliver.

As this is part of a conversation, the style is diffuse and informal. Charles will need to organize his notes, extracting the relevant information and arranging it clearly and logically. The headings and notation will probably be simple rather than complex, as the report is to be used as a discussion document, but this makes the need for close organization even greater. There are additional problems, such as placing the Latin names correctly and giving the references in full bibliographical detail.

In spite of the subject matter, the case study contains sufficient explanation of terms to make it a valid exercise for most students, whatever their specialism.

Minimum time allowed: 1½ hours

Transcript of Conversation

Charles:	I've not been to this part of Sussex before, but it's got all the right ingredients, hasn't it? You must have chosen it very carefully for your retirement.
Professor:	Oh I did, I did. As soon as I saw it, I said to my wife, we must find a cottage here, near the heathland with all those beautiful heathers and gorse, good open country, and not too far from the woodland, all those oak trees with sallow in the undergrowth, splendid food for the Purple Emperor and so on.
Charles:	You've even got a lake, haven't you? I thought I caught a glimpse of it as I turned off the main road.
Professor:	The lake was a real bonus. Hardly believed my luck when Ada, my wife you know, said there's a shallow lake down there, with more sallow round it. Absolutely wonderful. Lots of good camouflage, too.
Charles:	Yes, as I said when I wrote to you, that's what I'm really interested in. I should think you'd get both sorts of protection, cryptic species that merge into their surroundings in colour and

	shape, and the aggressive ones...
Professor:	Warning mode, I like to call them 'modes', cryptic and warning. Yes, I do see both modes... you know the Hornet Clearwing (*Sesia apiformis*) larva feeds on the poplars by the lake... it's got the common black and yellow colours of wasps and hornets, gives the birds a fright, and they leave the moth alone.
Charles:	It's about the size of a large wasp, the moth, isn't it? And doesn't it have clear wings, no scales like other lepidoptera? I suppose that's how it got its name.
Professor:	There's another one, very rare but I've seen it on the buddleias in the garden, same colouring, the Bee Hawk Moth. Not at all related to the Hornet Clearwing, but it's got clear wings too, and looks like a furry bumble bee. Stops the birds getting hold of it, they know that bees sting. Sometimes it's shape, not colour, of course.
Charles:	Yes. Have you seen the Elephant Hawk Moth, *Deilephila elpenor*? I noticed you'd got rose bay willow herb in the garden. The larva of that's fun, isn't it?
Professor:	Splendid creature. Yes, I saw it around there last summer. The larva swells up beautifully when it's disturbed, swells its anterior segments with big eye spots until it looks like the head of a snake. You know Ford's book, of course; there's something in that about the Elephant Hawk.
Charles:	Ford? Oh yes, E.B. Ford, *Moths*. Yes, I know that.
Professor:	You know he did *Butterflies* as well, don't you?
Charles:	Did he? No, I...
Professor:	Ten years earlier, 1945, same publisher, Collins. Useful books. Both in the same series... I can't remember...
Charles:	The New Naturalist Series? *Moths* is anyway, and I'll look out for *Butterflies* and see if I can pick up a copy secondhand. Thanks for the reference.
Professor:	Going back to the warning mode, in the woods here last summer I found something I never saw in London, the Lobster Moth, or rather its caterpillar, *that* uses shape, too. Extraordinary caterpillar. Lumpy, angular, draws itself up and rears up its end over its back to look like a scorpion. Butterflies do the same sort of thing, warning birds off, I mean... You know the common Peacock of course ...
Charles:	Yes, we get those at home, too, dark, unobtrusive until it's disturbed and then whoosh! all four red wings open with big eye-spots staring at you. Must be terrifying if you're a bird.
Professor:	The Eyed Hawk Moth, *Smerinthus ocellatus*, does something similar. Never seen one here, mind, though I saw plenty in my London days. Round here, though, the real beauty is the Purple Emperor. Caterpillar feeds on sallow, so it's a good place.
Charles:	That's certainly cryptic! I've never seen it, you know, though

	I've been for several years where it ought to be, but it never seems to be there when I arrive.
Professor:	I'm not surprised. I hunted it, man and boy, for twenty years or so. Ada used to say I'd got the thing on the brain. But it's worth it—come down here again mid to late July, and I'll find a butterfly for you. Emperor of the woodlands here, it is.
Charles:	I'd love to come back. Thank you very much. Why is it so very hard to find?
Professor:	Slug-shaped, just the colour of the leaves. The caterpillar of course... even has pale oblique stripes along its side, like the ribs of the leaf, and the slug-like horns at the head are like the leaf stem in shape and colour, especially if you look at it from the side. And the pupa is just the more delicate pale jade green of the underside of the leaf. You'd never see it hanging there....
Charles:	So I've found out!
Professor:	There's the caterpillar of the Lappet Moth, too, on the sallows down by the lake. I spend some of the best days since I retired at the lakeside, take a picnic, get out of Ada's way for a bit, sit and watch the most splendid blue dragonflies...and the Lappet Moth, I was saying, it flattens itself on the stem, same colour, same irregular outline, almost invisible. The moth's clever, too, has irregularly shaped purplish-brown wings, shot with light brown or gold, especially the second brood, which hatches in autumn. Holds its wings very oddly for a moth, looks just like a bunch of withered leaves...
Charles:	Out on the heath, I suppose you get the Silver-Studded Blue...
Professor:	Common, yes, common in early August. Has bright blue males and brown females, very inconspicuous. Just like the other Blues, Adonis and Chalkhill, but I don't see them here.... The Silver-Studded I often see, though, at least the males, which is the point, of course, the females are protected by their dark colouring...
Charles:	And males are expendable....
Professor:	Alas, yes. Among lepidoptera, anyway. You know the best bit of cryptic colouring I can think of?
Charles:	What's that?
Professor:	The Grayling. *Hipparchia semele*. The underside's grey and mottled, blends perfectly with the little stones and the sand among the heather. It's also programmed by nature to lean over into the direction of the sun, so it doesn't cast a shadow! Marvellous! You know I've seen this one when it lands, kept my eye on the place, gone very close, and still haven't been able to find it. I was so sure, I moved sharply and sure enough, the insect flew up almost under my hand. Marvellous disguise...

(The conversation was interrupted at this point by the arrival of tea.)

Case study 8   J.S. Morgan Ltd: a change in managerial style

Note

All students who have a managerial element in their courses will find this a useful exercise in report writing. It raises important questions about the relationship between senior management and workforce, and about the channels of communication within an organization.

J.S. Morgan Ltd (a fictitious name for a real company) has undergone a radical change in its management, from patriarchal to participative. The new Managing Director wishes to review the workforce's attitude to his innovations, and asks the Personnel Officer to prepare a report appropriate for discussion at a Board meeting.

The major difficulty in preparing such a report is one of procedure: clearly one cannot simply ask employees their opinions of the boss and his ideas! The report writer must therefore consider, preferably after thorough group discussion, how such information can be obtained. He will need to consider a wide range of sources, such as minutes of meetings, records of absenteeism and production figures, and assess both detailed comments and trends. Conclusions and Recommendations will vary, but must be firmly based on the evidence 'discovered'.

Minimum time allowed: 3 hours, with extra discussion time

Background

J.S. Morgan Ltd is an old-fashioned engineering firm, started in the 1920s by J.S. Morgan and taken over (with little change) by his son, R.S. Morgan, just after the war. The firm, as both Morgans liked to remind people, started in a couple of huts, with eight employees.

The Morgans were 'good' employers, generous with pay, bonuses, the 'personal touch'. Both boasted that they know all their employees by name and could ask after their families as appropriate. Nevertheless, with J.S. Morgan as Chairman and R.S. Morgan as Managing Director, decision-making was a 'family' affair, and there was no consultation with employees.

The firm prospered, and by the mid-1970s had a workforce of 600, most highly skilled, and a world-wide reputation for machine-tool engineering. Then J.S. Morgan died, and within a year his son retired in ill-health. No member of the family remained in the company. The new Chairman decided that the firm must radically change its attitude to its employees, and appointed as MD Michael Bridgen, a young, highly-qualified, go-ahead engineer. Michael had clear ideas about what he wanted—participative management and an 'involved' workforce. He persuaded the Personnel Officer, an older man but not averse to new ideas, to consider:

1. Three meetings a year of all active management and supervisors, with members of the Board invited, to take part in a 'question and answer'

session on company policy and objectives.

2. Fortnightly programme review meetings to discuss work in progress, with representatives of each function of the company down to and including supervisory level.

3. Contracts/production meetings at regular intervals to discuss completion dates, relations with customers, etc., and to identify possible difficulties.

4. Regular meetings of the Works Convenor and Senior Shop Stewards, with shop-floor representatives elected by the workforce.

5. Fortnightly foremen's meetings to discuss work problems and achievements.

6. One canteen for the whole workforce, although a private dining room to be available for working meals (available for any level).

7. A newsletter given to each employee four times a year.

8. Direct mailing to all employees if there seemed danger of misunderstanding which could lead to a dispute.

In the case of meetings (1 to 5), the MD could attend by invitation (or he could, by agreement, send one of his senior managers).

Obviously, not all of these innovations could be introduced at once, but after two years, most of them were at least in prospect.

The workforce seemed generally happy with the changes, but some older employees caused difficulties by constantly talking about the 'good old days', saying nothing at the meetings (but much in the canteen afterwards), and muttering about it being 'management's job to make decisions'.

Two years after his appointment as Managing Director, Michael Bridgen asks his Personnel Officer for a report on the workforce's acceptance of and attitude to the changes in managerial style. He would like to discuss the report, including any recommendations made, at the next Board meeting in about one month's time.

Case study 9 Cotham House

Note
The construction of a large office block always presents its planners with many problems. The project detailed below is for a building with an *insitu* reinforced concrete frame which is to fill the entire land available. Its structure means that large cranes must be used to lift panels into position but its base area results in limited space being available in which to place the cranes. Unloading, workmen's huts and materials storage all need space which is severely restricted in this case.

The information given below is a section (the Findings) of a longer report, detailing some of the problems caused by this construction. The facts are given without logical order or organization, and the writer is required to group together related details in order to produce a coherent structure with appropriate headings and notation. It can be assumed that the Introduction to the report will be written later, and that Conclusions and Recommendations are not needed at this stage.

In spite of the technical nature of the material, the case study can be undertaken by students of any discipline, although it lends itself most readily to construction and engineering courses.
Minimum time allowed: 45 minutes

Information
1. Cotham House is to have an *insitu* reinforced concrete frame and this, for practical and safety reasons, requires a full external scaffold. The minimum width will be 5 boards (1200 mm) plus flexibility for adjustment of 2 boards (400 mm).
2. The limited space means that materials will have to be moved frequently, when the storage area becomes required for construction. This movement must be minimized.
3. Maximum site occupation, including taking over the pavements, is required.
4. Part of the site is currently a car park for staff at an adjacent office block on James Street. Users must be given notice of its closure.
5. During construction, pedestrian access to the adjacent block must be provided. This should be a covered walkway to provide protection from falling objects.
6. Site accommodation of 189m² of offices, 54m² of canteen and welfare and 18m² of stores is required.
7. Cranes are the most expensive item and so the time they are required must be minimized.
8. Permission must be obtained from the owners of the adjacent office block for the cranes to use their air space.
9. Consideration should be given to the possibility of using three big cranes

outside the building and one small crane inside. It is not clear how the small crane could be removed when it is no longer required.

10. If there is sufficient space, forklifts could be used for some materials handling and lifting up to first storey level.

11. A building with an *insitu* concrete frame requires that the cranes provide lifting cover to 100% of the horizontal area.

12. Space is required for the manipulation of materials during the finishing and final internal completion stages.

13. Throughout the erection of the structure one concrete pump and at least one ready mix concrete delivery vehicle must be parked on site.

14. A minimum of two cranes is needed to handle the required amount of lifting.

15. The cranes should be outside the building footprint area, for ease of erection and dismantling. This will require the temporary closing of James Street.

16. If the crane size is increased from 52m radius, more flexibility to lift larger loads will be created. However, the next size range of cranes is far more expensive and so this may be uneconomic.

17. Adjacent road space is required for delivery vehicles waiting and unloading.

18. The Local Authority and the police must approve the site boundary and the taking over of pavements and parking bays.

19. Parking restrictions around the site must be revised for a period of 4 years.

20. The expected construction time is 180 weeks.

Case study 10   The Welfare of Pigs

Note

A research report on the behaviour of dry-housed sows forms the framework for this case study, which is concerned with the Discussion Section only of the full report.

At present, the information gathered is in the form of 23 observations, noted without any attempt to impose an order or to link related comments. These details should be organized logically, arranged under suitable sub-headings, and written up in formal English style.

Although this case study comes from the pure sciences, it may be undertaken by students of any specialism.

Minimum time allowed: 1 hour

Background

An enquiry was carried out into the effects of the confinement of dry-housed sows under the added stress of intermittent food presentation or deprivation. The objective was to consider the welfare of the pigs under the constraints of modern husbandry.

The pigs were studied for 3 hours at a time, with feeding every 30 minutes, over a 3-week period. All pigs were not fed at the same time, so that records could be kept of the reactions of 'fed' and 'unfed' pigs. Observations therefore show 'before feeding', 'after feeding' and 'interval' results.

Various behaviour patterns were recorded, together with any changes in behaviour resulting from the presence of boars and any changes which became apparent during the 3 weeks of the study.

The following observations were noted, and will form part of the 'Discussion' section of the final report.

1. Sows most frequently stand up after feeding and lie down before feeding.
2. Fed sows stand up much more than unfed sows. They stand to eat, and possibly remain standing in the expectation of receiving more food.
3. After 3 weeks, the sows remained lying down for much longer at a time. They had perhaps ceased to be disturbed by the presence of the observer.
4. Sow no. 7100 spent much more time with her eyes closed than any of the others.
5. Sows looked around at one another more after food had been distributed than beforehand. Unfed sows looked at their neighbours.
6. Sows which could not see boars tended not to look at other sows as much as sows which could see boars. Perhaps they showed competitive feelings towards other sows.
7. Both fed and unfed sows root in their troughs most frequently just after feeding time, perhaps to find more (some) food pellets.

8. Sows used the drinker press more frequently after the feeding time. This was true for fed and unfed sows.
9. Sows stood up as food was presented to them.
10. Sows generally had their eyes open immediately after feeding, but often slept during most of the 'interval' period.
11. Sows reacted to the presence of the observer most frequently between feeds, following him with their eyes.
12. Sows appeared to play with the drinker press as well as drink from it. Did it provide a stimulus for them?
13. Sows often stood up as neighbouring sows stood up.
14. Sows may drink in order to supplement an inadequate supply of food.
15. Sow no. 7100 stood up for only about one third as long as any of the others.
16. It appeared that sows facing boars looked more frequently at the observer than did sows which could not see the boars. It was possible that the sows looked past the observer, at the boars beyond.
17. Sows rooted in their troughs slightly less frequently as the 3 weeks of the study progressed. They did not appear to show any expectation of food.
18. After feeding, fed sows looked at the observer more often than did unfed sows. Perhaps the observer represented the food supplier.
19. Sow no. 7100 used the drinker press much less frequently than did any of the others.
20. Fed sows had their eyes open more often than sows which had not yet been fed. Perhaps feeding had provided more stimuli for them.
21. After 3 weeks, there seemed little change in the length of time sows spent looking at one another. The sample was perhaps too small to provide a statistically-accurate basis on this aspect.
22. The sows' reaction to the presence of the observer showed a strong negative correlation over time. During feeding, the observer moved towards the sows, which disturbed them. They watched the observer. As they became used to the observer, they were less likely to react to the observer's presence.
23. Sows which were not facing boars rooted the ground more frequently than the others. Were they reacting to a comparative lack of stimulus?

References

1. The Institution of Electrical Engineers: *Technical Report Writing* (Professional Brief by Joan van Emden and Jennifer Easteal) 1985
2. Buzan, Tony: *Use your head*, B.B.C. Publications, revised edition, 1982
3. Flanagan, Roger and Norman, George: *Life Cycle Costing for Construction*, Report published for the Royal Institution of Chartered Surveyors by Surveyors Publications, 1983
4. Turk, Christopher and Kirkman, John: *Effective Writing*, Spon, 1982

Bibliography

Barrass, Robert: *Scientists must write*, Chapman and Hall, 1978.

Booth, Vincent: *Communicating in Science: Writing and Speaking*, Cambridge University Press, 1985.

British Standards Institution: DD52: 1977 Draft for Development, *Recommendations for the Presentation of Tables, Graphs and Charts*, British Standards Institution, 1977.

Carey, G.V.: *Mind the Stop*, Penguin, 1971.

Cooper, Bruce M.: *Writing Technical Reports*, Pelican, 1964.

Gowers, Ernest: *The Complete Plain Words*, Pelican, 1970.

Kirkman, John: *Good Style for Scientific and Engineering Writing*, Pitman, 1980.

McKaskill, S.G. (ed. Joan van Emden): *A Dictionary of Good English*, Macmillan, 1981.

The Oxford Dictionary for Writers and Editors, Oxford University Press, 1981.

Weiner, E.S.C.: *The Oxford Guide to English Usage*, Oxford University Press, 1983.